A gift for:

From:

Faith

for a Lifetime

Daily Inspiration *for* Women of Faith

WOMEN OF FAITH

Celebrating 10 extraordinary years!

www.jcountryman.com
A division of Thomas Nelson, Inc.
www.thomasnelson.com

Published by J. Countryman, a division of Thomas Nelson, Inc,
Nashville, Tennessee 37214.

Compiled and edited by Terri Gibbs

All Scripture quotations, unless otherwise indicated, are taken from
the New King James Version (NKJV®), copyright 1979, 1980,
1982, Thomas Nelson, Inc., Publishers. Used by permission.

Other Scripture references are from the following sources:

The King James Version (KJV) of the Bible. New International
Version (NIV), copyright © 1973 International Bible Society.
Used by permission of Zondervan Bible Publishers. New Living
Translation (NLT), copyright © 1996 by Tyndale House
Publishers, Inc., Wheaton, IL 60189. Used by permission. The
New American Standard Bible (NASB) © 1960, 1962, 1963,
1971, 1972, 1973, 1975, and 1977 by the Lockman
Foundation, and are used by permission. The New Century
Version (NCV) ©1987, 1988, 1991 by W Publishing, Nashville,
TN 37214 are used by permission.

Designed by The DesignWorks Group, Sisters, Oregon.

ISBN: 1-4041-0051-2

www.thomasnelson.com
www.jcountryman.com
www.womenoffaith.com

Printed and bound in Belgium

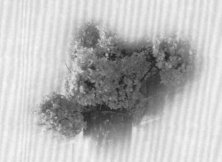

Faith
for a Lifetime

PREFACE

Hebrews 11 records stories of faith. Verse 13 says, "These all died in faith, not having received the promises, but having seen them afar off were assured of them." The men and women in the chapter were still living by faith when they died. They trusted God would keep His Word and He did.

Life offers abundant challenges as we deal with enormous "unknowns." Don't you often find yourself wondering what to do? Fortunately, God leads us every step of the way, and gives us wisdom.

One of the most remarkable things to me is that God cares about every detail of our lives. The life of His Son on this earth was amazing because He always did the right thing. And when He shed His humanity and returned to His Father, He left His Spirit to dwell within us and lead us through life, showing us "the right thing." Someone once said the Christian life is not difficult, it's impossible . . . we can only live it by faith, trusting the One who leads us every step of the way.

Stories of people trusting God inspire me. We find those stories in the Bible and in people like the ones who've written in this book—people who know God and take Him at His Word . . . people who have faith for a lifetime.

Mary Graham
President, Women of Faith

We stand firm in our faith
because it is our life.

January

We are designed like God—
fully human, fully alive.

LIFE WITHOUT MEASURE

*Nothing is better for them than to rejoice,
and to do good in their lives.*

ECCLESIASTES 3:1

God gave us life and vitality and a sense of wonder, and an enormous capacity to flourish emotionally, personally, and spiritually. Why do we often hold back? Why do we wait? Why are we afraid? Why not live fully and completely—regardless of the circumstances we encounter?

The most interesting people I know drink in life and savor every drop—the sweet and the sour. The good and the bad. The planned and the unplanned. And isn't that what God intends? When Jesus modeled humanity for you and me to see, He was out there—everywhere! He took risks. He embraced life and responded to everyone and everything, the tender and the tumultuous. His capacity for life was without measure. And we are designed like Him—fully human and fully alive.

Luci Swindoll, *I Married Adventure*

A DREAM FOR YOUR LIFE

The LORD your God has chosen you
to be a people for Himself, a special treasure. . . .

DEUTERONOMY 7:6

While traveling in the former Soviet Union and sharing God's "plan" of salvation with students, we never used the word *plan* since the Russians associated the word with the Communist Plan. We used, instead, the word *dream*, a close counterpart in their language. I remember talking with Svetlana, telling her God has a "dream" for her life. She lowered her beautiful face and asked shyly, "Does He know I am a Soviet citizen?" "Yes," I responded. "And still," she pondered, "He has a *dream* about my life?"

I assured her that indeed God has purpose for those who belong to Him. His purpose is to love us intensely and lead us intentionally into a broad place where we can know and enjoy His faithfulness to us. His commitment toward us is full of promise.

Mary Graham, *WOF Devotional Bible*

GOD'S LOVE LETTER

*I love the LORD, because He has heard
my voice and my supplications.*

PSALM 116:1

Do you remember receiving your first love
letter when you were in elementary school?
Your admirer may have passed it to you from two
rows over when the teacher wasn't looking.
Or maybe one of his friends hand delivered it to
you at recess. He poured out the depths of his
soul. Written in his best penmanship, these
unforgettable words were as sweet as a sonnet:

> I love you.
> Do you love me?
> Yes or no.
> Circle one.

God has written you a love letter, too. That
very special message is written in His wonderful
book, the Bible. Every word, every chapter, every
verse points to one central theme: God loves you
and invites you to have a very special relationship
with Him.

Babbie Mason, *WOF Devotional Bible*

REAL FRIENDSHIP

A friend loves at all times,
and a brother is born for adversity.

PROVERBS 17:17

Friendship is a wonderful thing. I cannot imagine a day going by without talking with my friends. . . . Ralph Waldo Emerson asserted that there are two cornerstones to friendship. One is truth, the other tenderness. I agree. To love someone, we must know they are truthful with us. Love is built on respect and respect on trust. Truth and tenderness must go hand in hand because if they try to stand alone, one will be too hard and the other too soft.

I would add a third element that is essential to friendship—freedom. We can love others tenderly, be completely truthful with them, but unwittingly want them as our own. We find ourselves hurt if they do things with other people and we're not included. If we don't encourage them to be free (even of us), there is no real friendship. When we hold on to anything too tightly, it dies.

Luci Swindoll, *I Married Adventure*

SMILE, CHUCKLE, OR LAUGH

*[He] works all things
according to the counsel of His will.*

EPHESIANS 1:11

That verse reminds us that God, in His
sovereign love and power "works all things
according to the counsel of His will." My security,
my rest, my peace, and my joy live always in the
sure knowledge of that comforting truth. But God
invites my participation in the executing of His
divine will for my life. To me, a part of that
participation has to do with how I perceive the
events of my life. I determine whether or not I'm
going to view my experiences through a negative
or a positive lens. If indeed my perceptions are
negative, then it stands to reason my life will feel
out of whack. Thank God I don't have to pout,
fuss, or complain; I have the option to smile,
chuckle, or laugh. When I do, in that arena where
God invites my participation, I am in control.

Marilyn Meberg, *Choosing the Amusing*

SIN IS SIN

*Though yours sins are like scarlet,
they shall be as white as snow.*

ISAIAH. 1:18

One of the great things about God is that He doesn't categorize sin. Sin is sin. No little sins, no big sins, just Sin with a capital S. All sin separates us from God if we don't have salvation through Jesus Christ.

The other marvelous thing about God is that He forgives sin and doesn't remember it anymore. No, there's nothing wrong with God's memory—but He chooses never to remind us of what we've confessed.

I don't know of a person who has avoided making an unwise, uninformed, unscrupulous decision. Sure, some of those decisions cannot be undone; we must live with them. There are consequences to everything we do or say. But through His Son, Jesus, God has made a way so that we can be forgiven, restored, and made whole again.

Girl, is that good news or what?

Thelma Wells, *Girl, Have I Got Good News for You*

LOOKING FOR PERMANENCE

*The things which are seen are temporary,
but the things which are not seen are eternal.*

2 CORINTHIANS 4:18

Whatever their circumstances, people in every land are searching for a reason to live. Someone needs to tell them, "This is it!" To know God and be involved in His plan for the human race is what the whole world is really looking for. They just don't know it yet! That's why they are looking in all the wrong places.

People are trying to find permanence as well. They are looking for a safe place to settle down, especially since the 9–11 tragedy. Travel to hot spots is down. Airlines are struggling, and tourism has taken an enormous hit.

We look for permanence, but the only permanence is eternal permanence—and only God can give us that! He is the only self-sustaining permanent being. God can give us eternal life and a permanent place to live in heaven if we ask Him.

Jill Briscoe, *Here Am I, Lord*

GOD GIVES ENCOURAGEMENT

But Noah found grace in the eyes of the LORD.

GENESIS 6:8

Noah surely felt strengthened as he walked with God and lived in His favor. How else could he have started such an outrageous project as building a huge boat in a desert nation where it seldom rained—when he was six hundred years old? Picture the old man struggling to coat the giant vessel inside and out with tar while his neighbors stood around the ladder, laughing and criticizing him. And then picture God holding the ladder steady and shouting up encouragement only Noah could hear: "That's it, Noah. Good job, son!"

In the same way, God's grace empowers us to do everyday acts of kindness and outrageous acts of courage on His behalf. Step out confidently on the path God sets before you, no matter how outrageous the goal may seem at the time. The God who steadied the ladder for Noah will hold you steady as you do His work today.

Barbara Johnson, *Women of Faith Devotional Bible*

GIVE UP YOUR WORRIES

*Blessed are those who keep His testimonies,
who seek Him with the whole heart!*

PSALM 119:2

Most of our days are filled with tasks we have to redo again and again. We wash dishes, only to wash those same dishes again at the next meal. We launder the same clothes over and over. We re-vacuum rooms. We re-mow the lawn. We re-dust our rooms. We re-wash our hair. We re-apply lipstick. Sometimes I wish the things I did would stay done!

These same kinds of maintenance issues come into play in our spiritual lives as well. We must read the Scriptures over and over. We must confess our sins to the Lord on a regular basis. And just when we think we have given all of our cares over to God, we find them sneaking back. That's part of being human. Don't be surprised if you have to deal with your fears and frustrations more than once. But don't feel defeated, as if you didn't get it right the first time. Deal with your heart before your worries can take hold again.

Christa Kinde, *Living Above Worry and Stress*

OUR MIGHTY RESCUER

By faith Abraham . . . offered up
his only begotten son . . . concluding that God was
able to raise him up, even from the dead.

HEBREWS 11:17–19

Do you see? Abraham believed God would bring Isaac right back to life. Wow! Though I don't have the faith of Abraham, there have been times in my life when one of our five children was in a situation I simply could not "fix," so I was *forced* to abandon that child into the arms of God.

When our son, John, was fifteen, he took up with a fast drinking crowd. My husband and I tried in vain to bring John to his senses. I had to abandon him to God. All I could do was fast, pray, and trust. Then, to my amazement, I saw God come running like a Mighty Rescuer. We "happened" to have a Nebraska football player stay overnight with us. This man loved God and stayed up with John until two in the morning. The next day John came to us, broken and repentant. Just as God rescued Isaac, so He rescued our son.

Dee Brestin, *Women of Faith Devotional Bible*

LIVING IN THE LIGHT

"I am the light of the world."

JOHN 9:5

Jesus says, "I am the light of the world." Keeping my eyes on Jesus, I can do anything. I can walk in light even on my darkest days.

Living in the light is one of the most difficult tasks we have. It means getting out of the way so there is no shadow blocking the source. The more light we live in, the more we grow and change.

Every day God reminds us to quit holding things too tightly—whether an event, a viewpoint, a desire, a particular time in life, or a person we thoroughly enjoy. He urges us to stop struggling, resisting, coercing, or manipulating for what we want. When we simply do what He asks, no matter how hard it seems, and we keep our focus on the Light of the world, an amazing brightness comes, all within the embrace of His love.

Luci Swindoll, *I Married Adventure*

You've Got to Let Go

Forgetting those things which are behind . . . ,
I press toward the goal for the prize
of the upward call of God in Christ Jesus.

PHILIPPIANS 3:13–14

When I was a little girl, my sister and I had been petting goats in our neighborhood park. One of the goats was hungry and became convinced that I was holding out on him. He stuck his head in my pocket and bit on something that smelled vaguely like food to him. He couldn't get his nose out, and he wouldn't let go. My sister told me to take off my coat, but I refused because it was my new green duffel coat. I ended up having to go home through the park with a goat attached to my coat.

When you won't let go of unforgiveness or bitterness, it will take you places you won't want to go. It will keep you tethered to an event that is long gone. Your heart will never be free until you let go.

Sheila Walsh, *The Heartache No One Sees*

A Foundation for Prayer

Let us therefore come boldly to the throne of grace,
that we may obtain mercy
and find grace to help in time of need.

HEBREWS 4:16

Some people would tell you not to ask God questions like, "Why?" I am not one of those people. I believe that asking God "Why?" indicates that we have the faith to know that He, and only He, has the answer. I believe "Why?" is a question that ultimately shows faith. However, once we ask the question, we must be willing to rest in His timing for the answer. For some situations the answer may come fairly quickly, for others, very slowly, and for some, not until we see Him face-to-face. If we trust in the sovereignty of God, we wrestle our way to peace in the knowledge that if an answer is for our highest good, the God who loves us will not withhold it.

Lana Bateman, *The Heart of Prayer*

WRESTLING WITH GOD

*Jacob was left alone; and a Man wrestled
with him until the breaking of day.*

GENESIS 32:24

Though I've never wrested with an angel in
the desert, I *have* wrestled with God. Tossing
in the night, I've asked questions like: *Why is our
daughter-in-law having miscarriages?*

One time I asked God, *Why is my sister so
closed to spiritual things?* He answered me not with
a question, but with a conviction in my spirit that
I was part of the problem. I had developed a chip
on my shoulder. My pride and my anger during
our spiritual discussions had shut her down.

The next morning I went to my sister and
humbled myself. I admitted my obnoxiousness.
I pled with her to give me another chance to be
the sister I longed to be. In the following years she
saw a change in me—and her heart softened
toward God.

As the great preacher Charles Spurgeon
warns, "If God Almighty is wrestling with
you, you'd better ask Him why."

Dee Brestin, *Women of Faith Devotional Bible*

GOD IS CRAZY ABOUT YOU!

*In his heart a man plans his course,
but the LORD determines his steps.*

PROVERBS 16:9, NIV

The principle truth that every woman has to grab hold of, whether single, married, divorced, or widowed is this: You are valuable just because you are you. God has plans for you just because you are you. You came into the world alone, you will leave alone, and you will give an account—alone. The relationships you develop along your life's journey may be highly significant and part of God's plan, but they do not define you. You are precious by yourself and God is crazy about you. He hasn't left you beside the road of life to languish while you wait for something wonderful to happen or someone wonderful to come along. He has plans for you, just as you are, just where you are.

Jan Silvious, *Big Girls Don't Whine*

FORGIVENESS

*Joseph said to them, ". . . You meant evil against me;
but God meant it for good."*

GENESIS 50:19

When confronted by little digs, false assumptions, malicious gossip, or blame shifting, our first impulse is to lash out, prove our innocence, and assert our rights. Nothing would make us feel better than to get even—to make our oppressors feel the same pain we have suffered at their hands.

Joseph's power over his brothers is poetic justice. It's ironic that their treachery would eventually put Joseph in a place to avenge himself. What would you have done in Joseph's place? His betrayers were at his mercy. They had ignored his pleading—now he could relish the sound of theirs. But no. As his brothers cowered in his presence, Joseph relented. He recognized the hand of God in his circumstances. Joseph set aside vengeance and chose forgiveness instead.

Christa Kinde,
Women of Faith Devotional Bible

DO YOU BELIEVE?

"He who receives Me receives Him who sent Me."

MATTHEW 10:40

In John 11:25, Jesus said to Martha, "I am the resurrection and the life. He who believes in me will live, even though he dies; and whoever lives and believes in me will never die."

Then He asked her a question: "Do you believe this?"

"Yes, Lord," she told him, "I believe that you are the Christ, the Son of God, who was to come into the world."

We can answer the Lord today. And when He asks again tomorrow, we can answer Him again. Our response will affect not only ourselves but those around us. Will we become embittered or empowered? Our decision doesn't affect whether He is or isn't. But He most certainly wants to hear our answer. He takes great delight in our trust.

Kathy Troccoli, *Hope for a Woman's Heart*

OUR OWN GOD

"I will take you as My people, and I will be your God."

EXODUS 6:7

As a child with seven older siblings, we only had bare essentials in our tiny house. My cousins, though, had everything . . . beds, rooms, TV, candy on demand, and space. Something about their house gave me a longing. On more than one occasion, I begged to spend the night with them. Inevitably I couldn't make it through the night. My uncle would have to take me home. "I can't stay here," I would cry, "I need people who belong to me." So home I went to crawl into a bed full of sisters.

There's nothing quite like having your own people. People who know and understand you, care about what concerns you, understand your idiosyncrasies. It's much better than "stuff." But that's nothing compared to having our own God. Belonging to Him is liberating. It sets us free and satisfies our longings.

Mary Graham,
Women of Faith Devotional Bible

LOVING OTHERS

*My little children, let us not love
in word or in tongue, but in deed and in truth.*

1 JOHN 3:18

Loving others can seem like such an obvious principle, yet we often fail to do so. I have found that when I actively love someone, it sucks the poison out of my heart. If it is a person that I don't really know, such as the clerk at the grocery store, when I show her love, I find myself caring more, seeing her through God's eyes. If that person is someone who was unkind to me, by actively showing them compassion and forgiveness, I find I have more mercy toward her, and that the irritation or hurt begins to be absorbed.

All this sounds so great and godly. As a matter of fact, it can also seem unattainable because of our human frailty. But the Spirit that raised Jesus from the dead lives in us. We can do all things. He will supply what He demands.

Dee Brestin and Kathy Troccoli, *The Colors of His Love*

LISTENING WITH THE HEART

Bear one another's burdens,
and so fulfill the law of Christ.

GALATIANS 6:2

We do two types of listening. One is listening for mere facts. With this kind of listening we hear words, process them, and internalize them. This is the kind of listening we do in classes, in business, or in committee meetings. We listen for information. The other kind of listening we could call empathetic listening. With this kind of listening we not only hear the facts—the words—but we also hear the heart and the soul behind the words.

I believe Scripture addresses specifically our need to be heard as well as our need to hear. Galatians 6:2 states, "Bear one another's burdens, and so fulfill the law of Christ." This verse speaks of reciprocity—I'll bear yours and you bear mine. How can we bear burdens if we don't listen to what those burdens are?

Marilyn Meberg, *Choosing the Amusing*

GOD CAN!

*Your hands have made me and fashioned me; give me
understanding, that I may learn Your commandments.*

PSALM 119:73

There are all sorts of reasons to feel inadequate.
One of the main reasons is that you are!
There are situations in many of our lives that are
frankly too much for anyone in the whole world,
so it's all right to look at it and say, "Here am I,
Lord . . . send somebody else." Of course there
might not be anybody else to send, and then you
have to decide what to do.

I've had my inadequate moments. Growing
up, I felt awkward and ugly in comparison to my
beautiful sister. I knew the boys wanted to get to
know me only so they could get to know her! We
feel inadequate a thousand times a day, about a
thousand different things.

The release comes when first you realize you
are indeed hopelessly inadequate, and then you
realize for this you have God! You can't; He can!
You are inadequate; He isn't!

Jill Briscoe, *Here Am I, Lord*

God Names You *Princess*

*In Your presence is fullness of joy;
at Your right hand are pleasures forevermore.*

PSALM 16:11

God draws near to our hoping, trembling hearts and whispers one word: *princess.* Heaven holds its breath as He speaks a name that is deeper than our gifts or abilities; a name that gives us our place and purpose in the world. For a woman, it is a portrait of her heart and soul, which belongs only to her and to no one else in the same way. It expresses the nature, the character, and the life purpose of the woman who bears it. To paraphrase George MacDonald, "Who can give a woman this, her own name? God alone. For no one but God knows and delights in who she is, and who she will become."

No one but God can recognize you fully. No one but God can love you completely. No one but God can name you Princess.

Nicole Johnson, *Keeping a Princess Heart*

SERVANTHOOD AND FRIENDSHIP

If we live in the Spirit, let us also walk in the Spirit.

GALATIANS 5:25

Regardless of your age you've probably run into people issues. Mine began in infancy when I bellowed for attention and folks didn't immediately sprint to my cradle. Know what I mean? Left to our humanity, we tend to be self-serving in how we relate and what we expect from others.

I'm thankful that Jesus set a new standard for relationships when He showed Himself to be a servant and a friend. Servanthood and friendship are excellent handholding, girlfriend attributes. It's hard to separate the two when one is longing for and working toward healthy relationships, whether that be mother-child, husband-wife, or employee-boss.

Patsy Clairmont, *The Hat Box*

God Is REALLY God

"For this purpose I have raised you up,
that I may show My power in you, and that My name
may be declared in all the earth."

EXODUS 9:16

A friend of mine read the entire Bible when she was twelve. When she finished, she said to her mother, "Wow! God is really, really God." What a statement! My little friend understood that God is powerful and accomplishes His purposes even when it makes no sense to us. He is strong and good, whether we recognize it or not.

And He is God. He's not afraid of being misunderstood by anyone. He always does what is right, in order to fulfill His purpose. The strength of that and His absolute sovereignty give me security. He is really, really God.

Mary Graham, *Women of Faith Devotional Bible*

REST AND REFRESHMENT

Take my yoke upon you and learn from Me . . .
and you will find rest for your souls.

MATTHEW 11:29

Freshness is a valued quality these days.
Women want to smell fresh, feel fresh, and be
fresh-faced. We use phrases like "fresh as a daisy"
and "let me just freshen up a bit." Advertisers have
latched onto this idea, and try to infuse their
products with appeal by saying they're fresh.
"Clean and refreshing!" "Minty fresh!" "Fresh as a
mountain breeze!" We buy air fresheners and
breath fresheners. We equate freshness with
lemonade, peppermint candy, morning air, iced
tea, waterfalls, and swimming pools.

Whether it's looking at your life through fresh
eyes, gaining a fresh perspective, or taking a refresher
course, every Christian needs to be refreshed
sometimes. God's Word offers daily refreshment
for our souls. God's people can refresh our hearts
by their love and encouragement. Rest in the
Lord. Refresh your Christian sisters!

Christa Kinde, *Living In Jesus*

"STAND IN THERE!"

Do not be afraid. Stand still, and see the salvation of
the LORD, which He will accomplish for you today.

EXODUS 14:13

I've often heard it said, in an effort to comfort
someone, "It will be alright. You just hang in
there." While those words do offer encouragement,
I'd like to look at it another way. To "hang in
there" paints a picture of dangling out of control,
of being vulnerable and exposed. I have childhood
visions of sheets and pillowcases flapping wildly on
the clothesline in my mother's backyard. At the
threat of a strong, summer afternoon rainstorm,
we'd rush to remove the fresh laundry before it was
ruined by dust or a family pet running for cover.

I choose to encourage others by saying, "It
will be alright. You just *stand* in there." Because
Christ was hung up for our hang-ups, we can
stand up with confidence, knowing that our
foundation is secure. Why "hang in there"
when you can stand still and watch God
work a miracle on your behalf?

Babbie Mason,
Women of Faith Devotional Bible

The Joy that Awaits

"In My Father's house are many mansions;
if it were not so, I would have told you.
I go to prepare a place for you."

JOHN 14:2

Once when Bill and I met with our insurance agent, he consulted some actuarial tables and told me my life expectancy was another nineteen years. The poor man probably expected me to be a little sad to hear this prediction. I was sad, all right, but not in the way he expected. As he delivered this bit of news, my face automatically wrinkled up into a frown, and I spouted off, "Ugh! I don't want to live that long!"

It's not that I'm living a miserable life. On the contrary, I've made it a habit to wring out of every single day all the fun and love I can find. Sometimes it seems I have the best of both worlds—overflowing joy here and the promise of eternal happiness in paradise. Still, I know that my pleasantest day here on earth is *nothing* compared with the unfathomable joy that awaits me in heaven.

Barbara Johnson,
Living Somewhere Between Estrogen and Death

The Lord Who Heals

"I am the LORD who heals you."

EXODUS 15:26

Fixing broken things is God's specialty. That wasn't His original area of expertise; creation was. But Satan, His created being, turned against Him, came into His garden, and brought deception, blame, shame, and brokenness. That was what Satan intended, but he underestimated God. Jesus would be His answer. He came to earth in human form to take away the sin and pain of His people. He would fix the broken places, heal and forgive.

If you are sick in spirit, Jesus wants to heal you. If your relationships are sick, He wants to bring wholeness. If your soul is damaged with discouragement, He wants to repair you. If your body is hurting, He wants to relieve your pain. His whole heart toward His creation is to heal us where we are hurt, because He says, "I am the LORD who heals you."

Jan Silvious,
Women of Faith Devotional Bible

God's Will Be Done

"Not as I will, but as You will."

MATTHEW 26:39

Jesus' last prayer before He faced the cross—
as He knelt in the Garden of Gethsemane—
is a critical prayer for us to examine.

*"O My Father, if it is possible, let this cup pass
from Me; nevertheless, not as I will, but as You
will.". . . Again, a second time, He went away and
prayed, saying, "O My Father, if this cup cannot
pass away from Me unless I drink it, Your will be
done"* (Matt. 26:39, 42).

In Jesus' prayer we see the most powerful of
all principles of prayer. While we may ask for
what we desire—and we should always feel free to
do so—ultimately, we must seek the Father's will
above anything we might want or ask. This prayer
is from the Son to the Father. It is every bit God's
prayer to God. In the very heart of prayer, we find
God's prayer, and in God's prayer we will never
be disillusioned.

Lana Bateman, *The Heart of Prayer*

HONEST BEFORE GOD

You shall know the truth,
and the truth shall make you free.

JOHN 8:32

I believe God wants us to be honest because He wants a real relationship with us, not something plastic or halfhearted. I sometimes ask myself how it must feel to be God and love people with a passion so great You would give Your only Son to hang on a cross yet day after day You see Your children hurting, but they only come before You simply to say, "Well, thank You, Jesus, for another day"? They never open up. They are never honest. How that must grieve God's heart!

I believe God much prefers to have His children come before Him and say, "God, this makes no sense to me. I hurt so badly. I don't think I'll ever understand, but, God, I love and trust You, and I rest in the fact that You know how I feel. I can't understand what is happening to me, but help me to glorify you through it all."

Sheila Walsh, *Life Is Tough but God Is Faithful*

FORGIVE OR FESTER

If you forgive men their trespasses,
your heavenly Father will also forgive you.

MATTHEW 6:14

When resentment is allowed to fester within us, we inevitably experience the physical consequences. Medical research has revealed that the connection between our emotions and our body processes is closely related. Resentment eats away at our insides in much the same way acid would. Many physical ailments such as headaches, stomach problems, colitis, and hypertension are nothing more than suppressed anger that has been translated into resentment.

St. Augustine said, "Anger is a weed; hate is the tree." Do I dare disagree with St. Augustine? I suggest that anger is not the weed, resentment is the weed; and if nurtured and cultivated by our minds, it will develop into tree-size hatred. God clearly demands that we forgive others as He has forgiven us. There's no way to get around it: forgive or fester.

Marilyn Meberg, *Choosing the Amusing*

February

God wants to fill our souls
with Himself.

TRUTH FOR ALL TIME

When He, the Spirit of truth, has come,
He will guide you into all truth.

JOHN 16:13

Every day I am more grateful for the one
truth—or certainty—that keeps being truth
no matter who or what challenges it. The truth I
taught my children when they were young is the
same truth that will guide them when they are
old. The truth became truth long before I spoke
it, and it will be truth long after I am gone.

At times I have blown it while sharing the
truth through impatience, anger, or doubt. But
the fault does not diminish the truth of the truth,
only the humanity of the truth-bearer.

In these times when the world proclaims the
absence of truth, it's more important than ever that
we discover truth through God's Word and then lift
it up to others. Like a maypole, the foundational
pole of truth will keep us from getting too far away.
It's our job to stay connected to it.

Lynda Hunter-Bjorklund,
Women of Faith Devotional Bible

GOD IS OUR GUIDE

For this is God, our God forever and ever;
He will be our guide even to death.

PSALM 48:14

Sometimes, they say, love's gotta be tough. I'll be honest—I had never reached the end of my emotional rope until my sweet little babies turned into teenagers. There were days when my husband and I didn't know whether to kick our kids out or lock them in!

When I didn't know where to turn or who to call for advice or help, I sought help from a perfect parent who had handled such things: I turned to my heavenly Father.

Knowing that our actions and reactions would ripple throughout our children's lives, my husband and I tried to pattern our actions and reactions after God Himself. After all, when we mess up, He chastises. He sets us straight, and sometimes He lets us follow our own foolish way…but He never cuts us off. He never holds grudges. And He quickly forgives.

Angela Elwell Hunt, *Women of Faith Devotional Bible*

GIVE GOD THE GLORY

The LORD of hosts, He is the King of glory.

PSALM 24:10

Being number one is very important in our world. The media keeps us posted on which movies are blockbusters, which books are best-sellers, which songs are the most popular, and which television programs are award-winning. We crown homecoming queens, judge beauty pageants, and host talent competitions.

It is easy to get caught up in this search for significance. We all want to accomplish something in our lives and be recognized for it. But in doing so, we are trying to gain glory for ourselves. The Bible reminds us that, in the end, there is only One who is worthy of glory. No matter what the polls and charts and nominations might be, in the end, all the glory belongs to God.

Christa Kinde, *A Life of Worship*

BEYOND HAPPINESS

The LORD will perfect that which concerns me.

PSALM 138:8

The happiness we desire so desperately in this life may not be what God wants to give us to "fill" our souls. He sees way beyond our circumstances. He can and will deliver a supernatural contentment and peace that is not dependent upon anything we may go through in this life.

Oswald Chambers said: "It is not our circumstances that matter, but God in our circumstances."

He wants to fill our souls with Himself. With His life. Happiness dries up. Eternal joy abounds forever. That gift is only found in Him.

That's Jesus. He is our hope. And . . . by the way . . . we do have a happily ever after. He promises it.

Kathy Troccoli, *Hope for a Woman's Heart*

WE CHOOSE GOD'S WAY

*"If you walk in My statutes and keep
My commandments, . . . I will give peace in the land."*

LEVITICUS 26:3–6

Have you ever noticed how some people who don't even know Christ can show character and wisdom in managing their lives and raising their children? Perhaps they seem blessed and at peace because they have stumbled upon God's ways.

Now, if He blesses those who unknowingly walk in His way, how much more will He bless those who give their hearts to Him and long to exercise His principles in their lives? When we choose His way, He blesses our land, meets our needs, keeps us from fear, and gives us peace. What more could we possibly desire?

Lana Bateman, *Women of Faith Devotional Bible*

RESTORATION AND FORGIVENESS

*"I will walk among you and be your God,
and you shall be My people."*

LEVITICUS 26:12

God told Hosea to go and find a wife. God then added the peculiar instruction that his wife was to be a prostitute. Hosea found a prostitute named Gomer with whom he fell madly in love, married, and had children. Gomer apparently found her life of being wife and mother stifling. There were no thrills in her present lifestyle so she returned to the old one. Heartbroken, Hosea raised the children and desperately missed his wife. After a period of time God told Hosea to find Gomer and bring her home. Hosea found his wife in all her debauchery and brought her back where he continued to love her and tend to her needs.

Hosea mirrors the constancy of God's love. He says in Hosea 14:4: "I will heal their backsliding, I will love them freely." Did Gomer deserve that kind of forgiveness? Do we? God's love extends beyond the limits of our sinful humanity. He longs to draw us into a state of restoration with Himself.

Marilyn Meberg, *Women of Faith Devotional Bible*

WE NEED EACH OTHER

The fruit of the Spirit is love, joy, peace, longsuffering,
kindness, goodness, faithfulness, gentleness, self-control.

GALATIANS 5:22–23

Sometimes I think I'd like to pack my bags, kiss my responsibilities goodbye, and move into a monastery. It would be a quiet retreat—a time of refreshment, refocusing, and revitalization. I could live a simple existence in my own little cloister room. Distractions done away with, I could go about the business of things pertaining to God. I could begin a prayer journal. I could study the Bible for hours, uninterrupted. It would be so peaceful. It would be so quiet. I like quiet.

Unfortunately, God hasn't called any of us to be hermits. We were made to need one another. A life characterized by the fruit of the spirit is a life lived in the midst of fellow believers. We need the gifts of the Spirit just to get along! Besides, it is our great love and care for one another that sets us apart from the rest of the world.

Christa Kinde, *A Life of Worship*

GOD SEES OUR NEEDS

I have indeed seen the misery of my people. . . .
I have heard them crying out . . .
and I am concerned about their suffering.

EXODUS 3:7

I love the way God not only sees people's needs, but He knows the right person to address that need. God isn't hampered by distance or circumstance, and He will work to bring the two together.

This happened in my own life. I was a student at college and fell ill one night. I was rushed into hospital and placed in a large ward next to the first Christian I was aware of meeting in so-called Christian England! I was the seeking soul. She was the willing worker.

How did God get us together? He used an event He had allowed in her life—an accident at work—to put her in the bed next to me. The placing and timing were perfect. I was frightened and open to being helped. She had the help ready and was willing for God to use her. She led me to Christ!

Jill Briscoe, *Here Am I, Lord*

DEFINING PEACE

The LORD lift up His countenance upon you,
and give you peace.

NUMBERS 6:26

Mankind defines peace as that moment when all of earth is without strife or war. If that were true, then peace would never find its defining moment here on earth, and the term most certainly would have disappeared from all human language centuries ago, an archaic dream. Peace, then, can only be defined by God, given by Him, and bestowed upon the heart as the crowning prize when every trace of our self has been surrendered to the Father's will. When all desire is lost in His, our life becomes a fertile plain—our heart the happy picking ground with peace the bounteous crop. It is upon this single plain of surrender that we can know true peace. It is the royal mark of our adoption, legally sealed by the blood of God's Son, Jesus Christ.

Patricia Hickman, *Women of*
Faith Devotional Bible

GOD IS SOVEREIGN

At the command of the LORD they remained encamped,
and at the command of the LORD they journeyed.

NUMBERS 9:21

I have seen an artist's depiction of the Israelites being led in the wilderness by the cloud of God's presence. The cloud was pictured as a huge, tall funnel that was visible to all. There could be no dispute about which path to take. When the cloud lifted, the Israelites marched, and when the cloud settled over the tent of Testimony, the children of Israel camped. They only journeyed when the cloud led them.

God guided and the people trusted. God knew the way they should go, and His plans were for their welfare. He was not distant, but ever-present to guide and protect them on their way to the Promised Land. Their part was to exercise their faith, be patient, and be ready to follow when the cloud lifted.

God has given His Spirit to guide us on our journey. He asks for our faith and trust, our willingness to wait for His timing, and our readiness to go at His command.

Cynthia Heald, *Women of Faith Devotional Bible*

GOD'S VISUAL LESSONS

*For lo, the winter is past, the rain is
over and gone. The flowers appear on the earth;
the time of singing has come.*

SONG OF SOLOMON 2:11

This morning I walked to my living room window and looked out only to discover hope in bloom. My magnolia bush was dancing in huge buds, several of which had stretched opened their petals to make show-stopping statements of Spring. They captured my attention and admiration.

What is there about new life that surges with expectancy? Do you think God knew we would need visual lessons written into nature for all of us to see and be reminded that even after a long severe winter we would eventually transition into a life-giving season?

Spring speaks of resurrection in a gazillion different ways and resurrection speaks of hope in its highest form. I don't know the winter that sends shudders down your spine, but I do know the Spring-Maker and He is close at hand.

Patsy Clairmont, *WOF Association Letters*

GOD'S POWER AT WORK

*"The things which are impossible with men
are possible with God."*

LUKE 18:27

Joy opens our hearts to see God's power at work in ourselves and in our world. It helps us to remember God's positive answers for all the negative things we say about ourselves, as shown in this wonderful list someone sent me:

You say, *"It's impossible."* God says, "All things are possible" (Luke 18:27).

You say, *"I'm too tired."* God says, "I will give you rest" (Matt. 11:28–30).

You say, *"Nobody really loves me."* God says, "I love you" (John 3:16, 34).

You say, *"I can't go on."* God says, "My grace is sufficient" (2 Cor. 12:9; Ps. 91:15).

You say, *"I can't do it."* God says, "You can do all things" (Phil. 4:13).

Barbara Johnson, *Leaking Laffs*

LIFE'S EBB AND FLOW

To everything there is a season,
a time for every purpose under heaven.

ECCLESIASTES 3:1

If you watch an orchestra carefully, you notice a couple of things. Though every seat is filled, not all the musicians are playing at every moment. As the conductor leads them through their music, some sections play, but others are at rest. When greater sound is called for, many are busy. When the softest movements are underway, a single instrument may have the spotlight. Yet all the orchestra members keep their eye on the conductor's baton.

The church is like an orchestra. We all keep our eyes on the Conductor, awaiting His direction. At times, we work hard, and the music of our lives is glorious. At other times, we are allowed to rest. Others take up the song. Life has that sort of ebb and flow. Whether you are giving your all right now, or are in a season of attentive rest, quietly waiting your turn, you are an important part of a larger group.

Christa Kinde, *Living Above Worry and Stress*

PEOPLE NEED PEOPLE

*"They shall bear the burden of the people with you,
that you may not bear it yourself alone."*

NUMBERS 11:17

Although I am an only child and have always
been very independent, I never was meant to
live life alone. Neither are you! Sometimes when
people fail to be there for you, it is easy to isolate,
to internally determine, "I don't need anyone. No
one can be counted on to help me." But that is
not the way God meant for us to live.

No one can mature and accomplish their life
purpose in a vacuum. No one succeeds without
the help of other people. No one learns without
interaction with other people, and no one can say,
"I don't need people."

The secret is to recognize that the people you
need are healthy, purposeful, positive spiritual
people. These kinds of folks make a difference!
When they impact your life for good,
you can pretty well know they are
heaven sent.

Jan Silvious, *Women of Faith
Devotional Bible*

ADJUST YOUR SAILS

*In this is love, not that we loved God,
but that He loved us and sent His Son to be
the propitiation for our sins.*

1 JOHN 4:10

As someone once said, we can't change the wind, but we can adjust our sails. How do we adjust our sails? By remembering what we know about God. We must be certain of who He is. We must be certain of His character.

When things happen in our lives that don't make sense and others want to accuse God of wrongdoing, we have to rest on His character and the history of His faithfulness. God may not explain. He may not reveal His plan. But He has revealed Himself. Everything we question about the hardships of life, it's injustices and it's tragedies, should be processed through what we know about Jesus Christ.

Kathy Troccoli, *Hope for a Woman's Heart*

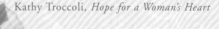

TRUE TO HIS WORD

*"Take now your son, your only son Isaac . . . and
offer him there as a burnt offering. . . ." So Abraham
rose early in the morning and saddled his donkey.*

GENESIS 22:2-3

As I read those verses, the most amazing words
to me are, "Abraham rose." Abraham was a
hundred years old when Isaac was born. God had
promised him that through this boy, He would
establish an everlasting covenant. Now Abraham
was being told to kill his son and offer him back to
God. When I try to put myself in his shoes, I realize
I would have left town quietly the night before or
pulled the sheets over my head the next morning.

Not Abraham. He got up. Why? Was he a
careless father, immune to the terror to which he
was about to subject his son? Not at all. Abraham
got up with the sun and saddled that donkey in
faith. You see God had a track record with
Abraham. God had always shown up at the right
time; He had always been true to His word.
Abraham's faith was based on what he knew of
God's character and God's ways.

Sheila Walsh, *The Heartache No One Sees*

GOD IS ALWAYS GOOD

*He has made His wonderful works to be remembered;
the LORD is gracious and full of compassion.*

PSALM 111:4

Life brings disappointment, disease, despair, and death. No one walks this journey without encountering rocky roads. Often life seems terribly unfair and inexplicable. Yesterday friends of mine lost their baby, less than twenty-four hours old. Why? They would have made wonderful parents, and they longed for this baby and prayed for him for years. Now he's gone, and their arms are empty.

At a time like this, the most important reality is God's sovereignty. Chuck Swindoll says, "God is not *almost* sovereign. He is in complete control of the circumstances of our lives. He is good. And He is full of mercy." He sees what we can't, knows what we don't, can do the impossible, and He is good. All of that, all the time. So we trust Him. In His greatest act of sovereignty and kindness to us all, He provided a Savior to forgive our sin.

Mary Graham, *Women of Faith Devotional Bible*

MORE THAN A CONQUEROR

*"In the world you will have tribulation;
but be of good cheer, I have overcome the world."*

JOHN 16:33

Jesus said, "In the world you will have tribulation; but be of good cheer." How outrageous! Be of good cheer when you have problems in your life? That doesn't make sense if you stop reading there. But if you believe the next statement, "I have overcome the world," it all makes sense. Jesus has the authority to declare that profound encouragement because He lived and died and rose again to make it true.

Dear friend, just as Jesus conquered death and has all power in heaven and earth in His hands, He will use His power to give *you* authority to triumph over any problem you are facing. Girl, you are not just a survivor; you are more than a conqueror through Jesus Christ!

Thelma Wells,
Girl, Have I Got Good News for You

THE CONSEQUENCES OF SIN

*I, even I, am he who blots out your transgressions,
for my own sake, and remembers your sins no more.*

ISAIAH 43:25, NIV

How utterly mind-boggling! God forgives the sins and then puts them out of His mind. And if it's out of His mind, He's not thinking up ways to dole out punishment. He's not thinking about the sin at all! Therefore He's not punishing at all.

"But," You say, "if God is not punishing me, why does it look and feel like punishment?" It looks and feels like punishment because we confuse *consequences* with *punishment.* God does not cause the consequences. Our behavior does. God is often blamed for what we set in motion when we sin. God is not responsible for our decision to sin. Neither is He responsible for the consequences of our sin.

Marilyn Meberg, *Assurance for a Lifetime*

SURRENDER THROUGH PRAYER

"Father, if it is Your will, take this cup away from Me;
nevertheless not My will, but Yours, be done."

LUKE 22:42

Jesus prayed, "Not My will, but Thine be done."
That's the most terrifying prayer in all of
Scripture. God asks some very hard things of us.
He asked Abraham to sacrifice Isaac; He let
Lazarus die before raising him from the dead; He
did not spare His own Son. God wastes nothing.
Not our joys, not our sorrows—nothing. When
we offer Him the essence of ourselves and we
submit to His work in our lives, His Spirit
produces character in us. He knows the fragrance
that comes from surrender. He knows firsthand
the return from the grain of wheat that falls to the
ground and dies.

I think we only get to this kind of surrender
through prayer. Just as Jesus did. We bring our
lives to Him and wrestle them to the ground and
let them go.

Nicole Johnson, *Fresh-Brewed Life*

THE HEART OF THE MATTER

*Then the LORD God called to Adam and
said to him, "Where are you?"*

GENESIS 2:9

"Where Are You?" Those three words
represent so much. When God called
out to Adam and Eve, He was after something.
He desired something. Something way beyond
what He was asking.

What God desired was honesty. He wanted
Adam and Eve to answer Him with the truth. He
desired for His children to realize where they
were. Tell Him where they were. That would be
their first step in realizing the state of their hearts
and their desperate need for Him.

I have learned that the Lord is always on a
pursuit to get to the heart of the matter. But we
keep changing the bandages instead of running to
God and saying, "Heal me, Lord—whatever it
takes." We hide and we keep on hiding. Like
Adam and Eve, God speaks to us: "Why are you
doing that? I see it all." He wants us to come to
Him with abandon.

Kathy Troccoli, *Hope for a Woman's Heart*

The Best Friend Ever

*"You are My friends if you do
whatever I command you."*

JOHN 15:14

How do you cultivate a friendship? It isn't always easy. First, you have to find someone who wants a good friend. Then, you have to find out about each other—personality, background, beliefs, likes, trustworthiness. It takes a lot of time to really bond, but over the course of months and years, friendship grows. There are ups and downs to share—listening, laughter, tears, encouragement, grief, prayers, misunderstandings, and forgiveness. Before you know it, you are giggling over private jokes and finishing each other's sentences.

We believers are offered this kind of close bond as well. Jesus called His disciples "friends," and He extends to us the same invitation. Wouldn't it be wonderful to leave loneliness behind forever, knowing that God is always near, always faithful, and always ready to listen? That's a friendship worth cultivating!

Christa Kinde, *Managing Your Moods*

I WANT GOD'S WILL

*Then the LORD opened the mouth of the donkey,
and she said to Balaam, "What have
I done to you that you have struck me three times?"*

NUMBERS 22:28

When you have "the want to" and "the how to" that match up with God's plan, you can know you are on target. And if you miss it, He is willing to do whatever it takes to reroute your path.

I learned a long time ago that I don't have to struggle with knowing what God wants in my life. If I want God's will, He will go to incredible lengths to see that I walk in it. If for some reason I don't want His will, He will work in me to help me come around to seeing it His way, because His way is always best for me!

So far, God hasn't had to use a donkey to speak to me, as He did with Balaam, but if He had to, He could and would.

Jan Silvious,
Women of Faith Devotional Bible

PEACE IS A POSSIBILITY

You will keep him in perfect peace,
whose mind is stayed on You, because he trusts in You.

ISAIAH 26:3–4

In a world that stands on the brink of wars and rumors of wars and the possibility of our cities being targeted for terrorist attacks, the question is being asked, "Where can we find peace?" Peace . . . the inner tranquility that lets me lie down at night and sleep soundly without worrying about anything. Peace . . . the hope that keeps me expecting all good things to happen. Peace . . . the assurance of knowing even if bad things happen, God has worked it all out for my good.

Peace is a possibility. In fact, God gave us peace. Peace is a promise from Jesus. Peace is a gift from the Holy Spirit. Jesus declared the Comforter, the Holy Spirit, would come to live in the hearts of the people when they received Him as Lord and Savior. The fruit of the Holy Spirit includes peace. When we place our faith in Christ, the Holy Spirit takes up residence in our hearts and brings with Him all His attributes, including peace.

Thelma Wells, *Women of Faith Devotional Bible*

SING GOD'S GREATNESS

Moses spoke . . . the words of this song, . . .
"Ascribe greatness to our God.
He is the Rock, His work is perfect."

DEUTERONOMY 32:1, 3–4

We frequently hear of Moses' ability to lead the nation of Israel, but we rarely hear of his ability to lead the singing. It was the same message, but Moses used a method to teach the faithfulness of God—he set God's principles to music. Moses wanted to remind us, as well as the people of Israel, if the Word of God is given first place in our lives, we will always be refreshed.

Have you forgotten how faithful God has been to you? Have you even taken Him for granted? Now is the time to count your blessings. Start by remembering that He has not forgotten about you. You are not an afterthought. Long before your mother gave you a name, God knew it. Before she held you in her arms, you were in God's heart. Your Father does know best. You and all of your concerns are taken care of. Remember that today, tomorrow, and always.

Babbie Mason, *Women of Faith Devotional Bible*

"It Is Written"

The word of God is living and powerful,
and sharper than any two-edged sword,
piercing even to the division of soul and spirit,
and of joints and marrow, and is a discerner
of the thoughts and intents of the heart.

HEBREWS 4:12

I love to sit in the morning in my favorite chair and read God's Word, meditating on everything I am reading, but there are times when I speak God's Word out loud as a declaration to the enemy that he has no place in my life, my home, or my family. We are told that it is sharper than a two-edged sword. It cuts through the lies of the enemy with the first strike forward and with the return back strike. The picture is that it shreds the enemy's attacks.

Do you feel as if he is coming at your family, your faith, your health, or your hope? Respond to the attack by declaring out loud the written Word of God. We stand with Jesus and say, "It is written . . . it is written . . . it is written . . . !"

Sheila Walsh,
The Heartache No One Sees

GOD GOES WITH US

"Be strong and of good courage; do not be afraid,
nor be dismayed, for the LORD your God
is with you wherever you go."

JOSHUA 1:9

Maybe because I'm the baby of the family, I like being "accompanied." Whether it's vacation or a trip to the store, you'll hear me say, "Want to come?" I drag people everywhere.

It's great comfort that God is with me wherever I go. His purpose is to stick with me. And mine, to stick with Him. I'm never alone. Sometimes I have to let His Word sink deeply into the recesses of my mind in order to remember, "Lord, thank You that Your Word says You will never leave me or forsake me. Even if I feel forsaken, You are here."

I meditate on verses like that night and day. When I do, I enter into God's perfect plan for my life—His purpose—which is for me to walk with Him, think like He thinks, do what He would do. He accompanies me through life.

Mary Graham, *Women of Faith Devotional Bible*

Shout Victory!

*All the people shall shout with a great shout; then the
wall of the city will fall down flat.*

JOSHUA 6:5

For six days, the Israelites followed Joshua's
instructions to the letter. Sandals slapped the
hard-packed earth, dust rose around their feet,
and the eerie wail of the seven rams' horns of the
priests filled the still air. The children of Israel
didn't speak—not even one word—until the
seventh day. Then after six long days of biting
their tongues and bottling up their words, the
command came. "Shout!" And with a roar, the
walls of Jericho crumbled. Victory!

Sometimes God asks us to have that same faith.
We face walls—circumstances we can't conquer—
and God tells us that we will be victorious. But then
all He asks us to do is walk—just trust Him with
the details, and keep on walking. Even when we
don't understand God's purposes. Even when we
can't see the point. God just asks us to have enough
faith to keep on walking. The victory will be His.

Christa Kinde, *Women of Faith Devotional Bible*

March

*We need the light of God
in order to walk in the ways of God.*

WHATEVER HE WILLS

So the sun stood still in the midst of heaven,
and did not hasten to go down for about a whole day.

JOSHUA 10:13

Science can't explain it. Reason can't deny it. Words can't describe it. How could the sun stand still and the moon stop until God's people had revenge on their enemies?

That's just the way God is. He is sovereign. He is free to do whatever He will . . . wherever He will . . . whenever He will to carry out His purpose and plan.

God doesn't follow the rules: He *creates* them. He doesn't worry about political correctness; He does whatever needs to be done to work things out for our good and His eternal purpose. You and I don't need to understand; we just need to follow.

Lynda Hunter-Bjorklund,
Women of Faith Devotional Bible

BASIC DOCTRINES

Blessed be the LORD your God, who delighted in you.

1 KINGS 10:9

Life is hard; no doubt about it. But in it there's lots of depth to be explored and growth to be experienced. That's all part of the adventure. For me personally, exploring, knowing, and experiencing life starts and ends with the fact that Jesus loves me. He tells me so. And it is that divine love that transforms the human heart.

I don't always get God's truth exactly right, and sometimes I'm way off, but I do believe a great part of my adventure in living is nourished at the well of having built my foundation on solid doctrinal truth. If we understand the basic doctrines of the church, even in a rudimentary way, we won't be forced to live according to our emotions alone. Our feelings will enter in, of course, and find their place, but we'll be able to stand on an unmovable, unchanging foundation we can trust.

Luci Swindoll,
I Married Adventure

THE LIGHT OF GOD

There is a way that seems right to a man,
but its end is the way of death.

PROVERBS 14:12

In *The Divine Conspiracy,* Dallas Willard tells of a pilot practicing high-speed maneuvers in a fighter jet. She became disoriented—thinking she was flying up a steep ascent—and flew straight into the ground. Willard says people without God are like that: they become disoriented, unaware that they are "flying upside down."

If you don't believe the absolute truths of God, and instead live by your own truths, you become disoriented, yet still take the controls, not realizing you are headed toward destruction. "There is a way that seems right to a man, but in the end it leads to death." We absolutely need the light of God in order to walk in the ways of God and to enjoy the abundant and eternal life He's promised.

Dee Brestin and Kathy Troccoli, *The Colors of His Love*

GOD'S GREAT PURPOSE

*Not one thing has failed of all the good things
which the LORD your God spoke
concerning you. All have come to pass.*

JOSHUA 23:14

If you are alive, God has a purpose for your life.
I am convinced He has plans for us beyond
anything we could ever imagine. His purposes for
you and me have been in His heart since before
the foundation of the world, and His concern for
us was viable and vibrant before we were ever
conceived. Not one of His thoughts toward us or
His promises to us has ever failed, nor will it.

When tough times come, sometimes it's hard
to acknowledge that His purposes are good; but
looking at your life thus far you will have to
admit, He always has been there and has taken
you to places you never dreamed you would go
and given you experiences you never thought you
would have. How great is that!

Jan Silvious,
Women of Faith Devotional Bible

GOD NEVER FORSAKES US

I will never leave you nor forsake you.

HEBREWS 13:5

Whether you are a traveler or a stay-at-home woman, you probably have your own sources of stress and chaos. Some of the most overstressed women these days are those who find themselves sandwiched between the exhausting job of tending their own children while also dealing with parents who are suffering health problems or slipping into dementia—and who sometimes live hundreds or even thousands of miles away. Throw in a full-time career and/or a husband who's dealing with a similar set of parent problems, and you've got the perfect launch pad for a trip to instant insanity!

When we're trapped in impossible predicaments we don't have a lot of choices. Our lives seem to be controlled by whatever blow hits us next, sending us lurching from headache to heartache to horror story. But we can choose how we respond emotionally. We can choose to hold on to the One who promises never to leave us, no matter how insane our schedules get.

Barbara Johnson, *Leaking Laffs*

WALKING GOD'S PATH

Teach me to do Your will, for You are my God.

PSALM 143:10

It was a miracle! The vast multitude of the Israelites walked through the middle of the Red Sea with their hearts in their mouths and hope in their hearts. They surely dared not breathe lest the waters close over their heads. So they were saved from the Egyptians.

The children of Israel could well have been happy with this state of affairs. Their victory had indeed been a great one, and the temptation was to stay and sing about it forever. But on the other side of the Red Sea, God instructed Moses to tell the people to go forward. He did not mean to go forward only to the other side of the problem. I am quite sure He meant them to go forward *ad infinitum*. To keep on going forward day after day and year after year. The Christian life is all about going forward, going on. The journey of faith is not a step, a leap, or even a plunge through the Red Sea. It is supposed to be a steady, daily walking along the path of God for your life.

Jill Briscoe, *Here Am I, Lord*

CAPTAIN OF OUR SHIP

*"Let not your heart be troubled;
you believe in God, believe also in Me."*

JOHN 14:1

God is the captain of our ship as we sail through storm-tossed seas. His Word is the lighthouse, to protect us from the hidden rocks beneath the dark waters. Ignoring the lighthouse, or "grabbing" the wheel from His capable hands, will lead to destruction. We will surely crash into the rocks and find ourselves sinking.

Often we have no idea where He is taking us. I know I will often look out at the stormy sea of life and say, "I'm so glad You know where You're going, God, because I'm completely lost."

We can trust His heart. He knows where He wants to take us. He knows what is right for us. Let's let Him get us home without a fight. And He will get us home.

Kathy Troccoli,
Hope for a Woman's Heart

PRAYER GOD'S WAY

*Ask, and it will be given to you; seek,
and you will find; knock, and it will be opened to you.*

LUKE 11:9

One time when Jesus was teaching about prayer, He used the example of someone running to a friend at midnight and asking for bread to feed an unexpected guest. It seems the friend didn't even come to the door, but shouted from inside the house: *"The door has already been shut and . . . I cannot get up and give you anything"* (Luke 11:8–8).

Until recently, I believed this passage meant that I was to storm the gates of heaven for anything important to me. However, the Lord showed me that this passage is a contrast between the ways of the world and the ways of heaven. The friend who refused to get up unless hounded to death is a picture of how the world deals with human needs. If we beg and make ourselves obnoxious, the chances are better that we will finally have what we ask. Jesus then described the Father's way. Simply ask and it will be given to you.

Lana Bateman, *The Heart of Prayer*

GOD'S HEART IS LOVE

It was right that we should make merry and be glad,
for your brother . . . was lost and is found.

LUKE 15:32

Remember the story of the prodigal son? This ungrateful twit asked his father for his inheritance money early—which was not done in that culture—but his father gave it to him anyway. In a faraway country, the son lost his inheritance on wine, women, and song. He had nothing left— and no way to take care of himself. He thought, *"I'm going home. Maybe my father will receive me as a servant."*

The father was watching one day, when he saw his tattered son returning home. He picked up his robes and ran toward his son, embraced him, and gave a huge welcome-home dinner. According to custom, the boy should have been disowned.

Jesus told the story of the prodigal son so we would know that God watches the horizon for each of us when we repent and return home. The nature of God is to give second, third, and 999 chances because His heart for us is love.

Marilyn Meberg, *Overcoming Mistakes*

A ROBE OF RIGHTEOUSNESS

"Fear the LORD, serve Him in sincerity and in truth, and put away the gods which your fathers served on the other side of the River and in Egypt. Serve the LORD!"

JOSHUA 24:14

My three-year-old is at the stage where he likes to dress himself. Every morning he'll choose a mismatched ensemble from his drawers and pull it on right over his footed pajamas. He'll arrive at breakfast in bulky layers, only to be sent back upstairs to set things right.

Sometimes we do the same thing. We try to hang on to our favorite pj's when the Lord is asking us to trade them in for a robe of righteousness. Joshua needed to urge the children of Israel to put away their false gods. If you were truthful with yourself—and with God—would you need to put away something as well?

Christa Kinde, *Women of Faith Devotional Bible*

TWICE LOVED

I have loved you with an everlasting love.

JEREMIAH 31:3

I once heard a Jamaican missionary tell the familiar story about a little boy who built a beautiful boat. When the boy took his masterpiece out for a test run, it sailed away from home. He lost his prize.

Time passed, and the little boy saw his boat displayed in a store window. He opened the heavy door, ran to the counter, and said, "You found my boat! Please give me back my boat!" "Give me two dollars," the clerk said "and the boat is yours."

The boy hurried home and worked odd jobs. Finally he counted, "$1.98, $1.99, $2.00." He went back to the store. With two dollars' worth of change on the counter, the clerk handed over the boat. The boy clutched it to his chest and said, "Little boat, little boat, twice I have loved you. First I made you; now I have bought you."

We're like that little boat. God made us, then He bought us through the death of His Son. We are twice loved.

Lynda Hunter-Bjorklund, *Women of Faith Devotional Bible*

A Good Man Will Wait

*"Sit still, my daughter, until you know
how the matter will turn out."*

RUTH 3:18

In every great love story there is an obstacle. Boaz, a good man, loved Ruth and longed to marry her. The problem was, according to the law, someone else was first in line. Widows were destitute in those days, but a near relative could purchase the land a widow lost when her husband died, marry her, protect her, and provide for her. Boaz was a relative, but the other guy was a nearer relative, and he was a cad! He wanted the land, but cared nothing for Ruth. If Ruth had hurried into this marriage, she might have ended up with the cad, but she listened to Naomi's advice.

How many young women have failed to listen to their parents or godly older mentors, hurried into marriage, and then had great regrets? Character can only be revealed by time. Don't panic. If God is in it, He will keep it together. Trust God enough to give it time. A good man will wait.

Dee Brestin, *Women of Faith Devotional Bible*

DON'T BORROW TROUBLE

*Do not worry about tomorrow,
for tomorrow will worry about its own things.
Sufficient for the day is its own trouble.*

MATTHEW 6:34

When I take only one day at a time, life looks like a piece of cake! But more often than not, my mind is stretching forward, and I begin to worry about my tomorrows. Don't you? I hope it doesn't rain for Saturday's game. I hope my new boss isn't a tyrant. What if the house burns down? What if the plane crashes? I wonder if we have enough life insurance? What if I lose my job? What if it's cancer?

Sure we need to plan ahead, but don't go borrowing trouble from tomorrow! If we allow our stomachs to roil over all the possibilities the future may hold, we'll make ourselves absolutely sick. Jesus wasn't kidding when He said not to worry about tomorrow because today has enough worries of its own. It's a good start on managing our anxious moods.

Christa Kinde, *Managing Your Moods*

GREAT THINGS HE HAS DONE

*Fear the LORD, and serve Him in truth
with all your heart; for consider
what great things He has done for you.*

1 SAMUEL 12:24

Remember this about God: "Great things He
has done for you." That one truth will take
you a long way on a bad day.

I spoke with a woman whose husband died
suddenly. She was shocked, but I remember one
thing she said: "God has done great things for me
in the past; He will not let me down now." She
remembered what He had done, therefore she
could go forward.

You can go on with great confidence, too, if
you will consider the great things the Lord has
done for you.

Jan Silvious, *Women of Faith Devotional Bible*

LET'S GET REAL

*Come to Me, all you who labor
and are heavy laden, and I will give you rest.*

I spent so many years in ministry trying to show what it would look like if someone sold out to God. Now I know that my apparent perfection left a gulf between me and other people. My open brokenness was the first bridge that allowed people to cross over and come to me.

It's hard to admit helplessness over our behavior and to ask for help. But I don't want to live in the chains of pride and fear. I want to find healing and to share life with other believers. Admitting our need for help to quit being victims or abusers or hypocrites can free us and the generations to come. I want to live with real people. And I want to be real, too.

Perhaps some of us walk with a limp. Perhaps we will always have scars. The One we follow has carried His scars for a long time, and He longs for us to show Him ours so He can heal them.

Sheila Walsh, *Life Is Tough but God Is Faithful*

SING!

Whenever the spirit from God was upon Saul, . . .
David would take a harp and play it with his hand.
Then Saul would become refreshed and well.

1 SAMUEL 16:23

Have you ever been to a bridal shower or a baby shower? Most of us have. Showers are a chance to dust off the punch bowl and make fussy foods. Pastel colors reign in the decorations, and a table stands ready to receive the mountains of presents. Often the hostess will pass out index cards and pencils and say something like, "Write down your advice to the new mom," or "Impart some wisdom from your vast experience to this new bride." A daunting task! But a few years back I hit upon my favorite tidbit of advice. Sing! Sing around the house. Fill your home with the sounds of rejoicing. Just as David's music healed Saul's troubled spirit, so music will soothe a troubled soul today. It will lift your heart into the heavenlies even as your hands are busy about the tasks of home.

Christa Kinde, *Women of Faith Devotional Bible*

THE BIGGER PICTURE

His compassions fail not.
They are new every morning; great is Your faithfulness.

LAMENTATIONS 3:22–23

When a parent has a new baby, it is necessary to have that little one immunized against deadly diseases. At just a few weeks old, the baby is taken to the doctor and placed in the hands of one who will inflict the worst pain this child has ever experienced. If the infant could speak in those moments when the needle enters the leg, the words might be, "Why have you done this to me? You have given me to a stranger and let him hurt me. You couldn't love me and let me suffer like this." However, the parent sees the bigger picture, what the baby cannot see. The pain of the moment may ultimately save the child's life.

When we look at God's sovereignty from this perspective, it can dramatically change how we live. Our peace comes from knowing that the God who loves us allows not always what feels good, but what is ultimately the very best for us!

Lana Bateman, *Women of Faith Devotional Bible*

GOD'S WAY IS PERFECT

As for God, His way is perfect.

2 SAMUEL 22:31

A funny thing happens when we choose God's way over ours: Our way becomes perfect—perfect in its purpose and perfect in its plans. No, we won't always escape the long nights or bad phone calls; we won't walk through life with only clean health reports and paid bills. But God will be a shield around us, protecting us from the pain of life, underlining the joy in all things. He is sovereign God over all—our strength and our power. What could be more perfect than that?

Karen Kingsbury, *Women of Faith Devotional Bible*

No Average Days

Through God we will do valiantly,
for it is He who shall tread down our enemies.

PSALM 60:12

I read once, "The pessimist may be proved to be right, but the optimist has a better time on the trip." How true!

What if everybody in the whole world decided to start looking at life through the lens of possibility? There would be no boring people. There would be no average days. . . . There would be no reason for prolonged discouragement—nothing to hold us back from conquering the enemies that steal our joy or disturb our souls. Everything would be possible because our focus would be on the Lord Jesus, who makes all things possible and is Himself the Master of adventure. It is He who is in charge of the voyage and asks us to capture the moment as He guides the boat. Think of the stories we'll have to tell at dinner.

Luci Swindoll, *I Married Adventure*

JESUS CALMED THE SEA

He arose and rebuked the wind,
and said to the sea, "Peace, be still!" And the
wind ceased and there was a great calm.

MARK 4:39

Remember when the disciples were out in a storm with Jesus? They were terrified of the waves and the lightning. The Sea of Galilee is capable of great fury, and the waves, we are told, threatened to overturn the boat.

In their panic they awakened Jesus. They called on Him to do *something*. Surely this great Man could pray—He seemed to have such a connection with the Father. Or surely He could give them instructions so the boat would not sink—He seemed so very wise.

Instead, Jesus did what He often does—He responds in ways that make us stand in awe of Him, causing us to realize that we are dealing with God Almighty. He stood up and told the sea to be calm.

Dee Brestin and Kathy Troccoli,
The Colors of His Love

DAUGHTERS OF THE KING

Commit your way to the LORD, trust also in Him,
and He shall bring it to pass.

PSALM 37:5

When we have a problem trusting, we don't need to brush up on the rules of how to trust; we need to get better acquainted with the One we are trying to put our trust in. When a woman sees a doctor about a heart condition, she listens to what the doctor says about how to lower her cholesterol. If she believes him, she trusts him. She will not say, "No butter? You won't let me have any butter? Listening to you is just about following rules." What the doctor says means something to her, and what the doctor is telling her to do is what is best for her heart. She trusts that the doctor's intentions are good toward her and that his goal is to take care of her.

God loves us more than any doctor. We can take Him at His word. . . . He loves us and cherishes us. We can hold our heads high as daughters of the King, loved by the greatest Prince of all time.

Nicole Johnson, *Keeping a Princess Heart*

REACH OUT WITH LOVE

*May the LORD our God . . . incline our hearts
to Himself, . . . that all the peoples of the earth may
know that the LORD is God.*

1 KINGS 8:57–60

So you cannot give some great theological
treatise. So you cannot read Greek or Hebrew.
So you don't know your "isms" from your "ologies."
So what! Very few of us will ever be great orators.
Not everyone is prepared to debate the finer points
of doctrine. And that's okay!

God uses the simple things of the world to
confound the wise. In other words, He can take
our everyday routines, our ordinary circumstances,
and our simple faith to change lives. Don't let fears
and uncertainties get in the way of showing God's
love. Reach out to those around you. Tell them
about your own experiences. God will use your
kindness and unselfishness to capture the attention
of the lonely and lost. Be matter-of-fact about
God's love, grace, and forgiveness. And relax. You
can't mess up eternity for them. We can just share
from our hearts. Only the Spirit can change theirs!

Christa Kinde, *Women of Faith Devotional Bible*

LIBERATING GRACE

God is able to make all grace abound toward you, that you . . . may have an abundance for every good work.

2 CORINTHIANS 9:8

I'm so grateful Jesus enables me to change, one groaning effort at a time, and I'm thankful for those folks in my life who have given me the space and time to change. It's easy (but not loving) to view a person in one light and mentally lock that person into never being different.

Grace is a liberating quality—no, let me restate that. Grace is a required quality for family members, mates, moms, servants, and friends. Grace is a wide space, acreage full of forgiveness, humility, acceptance, safety, and love. When I consider what great things the Lord has done for me, grace and friendships make me want to break out bags of confetti, kazoos, and my most outrageous party hat!

Patsy Clairmont, *The Hat Box*

LET GOD DO IT

*In all these things we are more than conquerors
through Him who loved us.*

ROMANS 8:37

The love of God is the key to trusting Him enough to let Him "do it." Do what? Everything! Absolutely everything. The joy of responding to God's love for us comes in the partnership He offers us in overcoming our difficulties. We are not alone in them. He partners with us by providing the wisdom and strength—and even abstinence from those life issues that threaten to derail us. In our love for Him, in our trust of Him, we receive from Him all we are not. This is what it means to "let Him do it." He invites us to climb off the treadmill of self-effort and rule keeping.

God plays the major role while we rest in who He is and what He has done and in the knowledge that we were, are, and will always be the focus of His love. And that powerful love is what brings us from death to life.

Marilyn Meberg, *Assurance for a Lifetime*

THE STILL, SMALL VOICE

Your ears shall hear a voice behind you, saying,
"This is the way; walk in it."

ISAIAH 30:21

Some years ago I was struggling with a congenital foot problem. I prayed about what to do, and with each prayer I had a knowing in my spirit that I should go to a podiatrist, a simple foot doctor. However, when the time came to take action, I felt my situation would be better served by a more educated, orthopedic surgeon.

After extensive surgery, I found myself with eight missing bones, toes sewn together, and problems that would last a lifetime. Disheartened and discouraged, I was now willing to go to the podiatrist. He looked at my feet with amazement and said, "Who did this to you?" He explained that all the toes had required was a simple cutting of the tendons and splints to hold them straight for a few weeks. I was stunned and angry!

Look what I had brought on myself by not heeding the simple prodding of the Spirit in my heart.

Lana Bateman, *Women of Faith Devotional Bible*

WORDS OF LOVE

Love . . . is kind.

1 CORINTHIANS 13:4

I have learned that if I don't give access to the truths of God to enter my heart, many other "voices" will get my attention. Especially in times of crisis. We are so vulnerable. We can easily despair and feel hopeless. Our emotions are tossed back and forth like ping-pong balls. One day we're "fine." The next day we're "losing it." Even when we don't have the strength to read, or to put "good" things into our souls, we must somehow allow words of life to be spoken over our loved ones and ourselves. Obviously, the source of life is Scripture, but words of love could also come from a lovely book, a sweet card, or an encouraging letter. A prayer from a fellow believer could also be what blows a breath of life into our deflated hearts. The Lord comes in so many wondrous and miraculous ways. It's just that He doesn't always come in ways we expect.

Kathy Troccoli,
Hope for a Woman's Heart

Just a Prayer Away

I will lift up my eyes to the hills—from whence comes my help? My help comes from the LORD, who made heaven and earth.

PSALM 121:1–2

The best way to get outside yourself is to keep looking up to God, the Author and Finisher of your faith. He is the only Person who will be with you every second of every minute of every hour of every day for the rest of your life. He is as close as the air you breathe. Nothing escapes Him. He is the only Person who completely knows how you feel and why you feel that way.

Psalm 121:1–2 is such a powerful proclamation: "I will lift up my eyes to the hills—from whence comes my help? My help comes from the LORD, who made heaven and earth." Read and digest that entire psalm, my friend. Every time you start to get down in the dumps, meditate on those words. Start right now, Baby. Proclaim out loud, "My help comes from the Lord!" Or just say, "HELP ME, JESUS!" He will. He's always just a prayer away.

Thelma Wells, *Girl, Have I Got Good News for You*

THROUGH ALL ETERNITY

We, according to His promise, look for new heavens
and a new earth in which righteousness dwells.

2 PETER 3:13

Sometimes, for a change of pace, I go through the day savoring the idea of eternity. Of course I don't really know exactly what heaven will be like, but that's okay. There are numerous Bible verses telling me about it and I have a picture of it in my mind. I know it will be wonderful. I know it will exceed even my best imaginations. And I know it will never end. That fact alone blows my away!

Just for fun, I carry in my billfold two fortune cookie "prophecies" I love. I have saved them for years as reminders to celebrate both the here and now and the up and coming. One says, A LITTLE MADNESS, A LITTLE KINDNESS,MAKES FOR HAPPINESS and the other says, AN INHERITED TREASURE AWAITS YOU.

Luci Swindoll,
You Bring the Confetti

THE BONDS OF MATRIMONY

A cord of three strands is not quickly broken.

ECCLESIASTES 4:12

Even though we poke fun at husbands and their different way of doing things, most of us have chosen to link our lives with theirs and face whatever comes, good or bad, laughter or tears.

Entangled is the perfect word for couples tied to each other by the bonds of matrimony. Sometimes we're wound up and crisscrossed like contestants playing the old Twister game. And at other times, it feels as if we're irreparably stuck in one big knot. But without that tangled knot, I know for sure I'd be at loose ends, because there's a third strand running through our marriage that ties us, not only to each other, but also to our Creator. That strand is God's love for us.

Barbara Johnson, *Leaking Laffs*

OUR CONSTANT COMPANION

Lo, I am with you always, even to the end of the age.

MATTHEW 28:20

When I was a child, I had my little fears. When day was done, I needed certain reassurances at bedtime. One was my teddy bear, ingeniously named Teddy. Then there was my nightlight. I could see it's orange glow from my bed, and it comforted me.

Did you know the children of Israel had nightlights? The entire nation was afraid in the dark. In ancient times, the oil lamps that lit homes were kept burning all night long. It was so important to keep that lamp burning that poor people would spend their money on oil first, even if there wasn't enough money to buy food! God knew His people needed certain reassurances. So when they were uprooted from their homes and forced to pitch their tents in barren landscapes each night, they were comforted by the presence of a pillar of fire. The glow it cast over the sleeping camp reminded the children of Israel their Constant Companion was near.

Christa Kinde, *Living Above Worry and Stress*

WORSHIP OR WORRY?

Let us continually offer the sacrifice of praise to God,
that is, the fruit of our lips, giving thanks to His name.

HEBREWS 13:15

In 1991 I spent some time with Ruth Bell Graham in the Grahams' lovely mountain home in North Carolina. Mementos of years of faithful service to Christ across the globe and in her home surround her there. Pictures of her children, grandchildren, and great-grandchildren adorn every tabletop. She's the mother of five, grandmother of nineteen, and great-grandmother of three.

I asked Ruth how she handled the tough days as a young wife and mother. How did she respond when she was, at times, pushed into the unsolicited spotlight? Her answer was simple yet profound.

"Worship and worry cannot exist at the same time in the same heart," she said. "They are mutually exclusive."

Sheila Walsh, *Life Is Tough but God Is Faithful*

April

If you want to get
God's full attention, praise Him.

TRUE FRIENDSHIP

Greater love has no one than this,
than to lay down one's life for his friends.

JOHN 15:13

Mother told me once when I wanted to give up
on a friendship that wasn't going my way to
look at it from the other person's point of view. She
said something like, "You can't make people into
what you want them to be. People are themselves.
Try to think about what you can give them, not
what they can give you." That was good advice.

True friendships are characterized by grace,
truth, forgiveness, unselfishness, boundaries, care
and love in gigantic and mutual proportion.
Although they require hard work and consistency
from each party, we enjoy the best of the best in life
because when friends come alongside, more light is
added to our path. We lay down our lives for our
friends, they lay down their lives for
us, and in the end we all find
true life.

Luci Swindoll,
I Married Adventure

WALKING IN TRUTH

I have walked before You in truth and with a loyal heart, and have done what was good in Your sight.

2 KINGS 20:3

A sweet friend, who had moved to another city, expressed a desire to come and visit in my home when she was in town. While I had opened my home to her, I knew I couldn't have her visit when I was traveling throughout the year. It became clear as time went by that she wanted to come every month or so, and she didn't see the need for me to have those few days alone each week. Now, when my friend would call and say that she was coming, I would get very irritated at her thoughtlessness.

Well, it all came to a head on her last visit when we sat down together and spoke our hearts. I found that she had been deeply hurt and shed many tears because I had become so distant and irritated. As I asked her forgiveness, I realized I had caused all of this pain by not walking in truth before my friend and before the Lord. Healing can't come until truth does!

Lana Bateman, *Women of Faith Devotional Bible*

The Final Say

Yours is the kingdom, O LORD,
and You are exalted as head over all.

1 CHRONICLES 29:11

There's no such thing as a self-made man—
or woman, for that matter. All that we are
and have—talents, skills, appearance, health,
upbringing, money, experiences—comes from
God. And God has the final say about whether it
amounts to a little or a lot. He can create the
right circumstances and control the outcome so
that we experience great results and rewards.

Nothing falls outside His control. Not jobs.
Not layoffs. Not relationships. Not finances. Not
governments. Not leaders. Not war. Not weather.
Not economic collapse. God's power and control
are absolute. Within that knowledge lies great calm.

Dianna Booher, *Women of Faith Devotional Bible*

Tell God About It

Be anxious for nothing, but in everything
by prayer and supplication with thanksgiving let your
requests be made know to God. And the
God of peace will guard your hearts and your minds.

PHILIPPIANS 4:6–7

Anxiety does you no good. It only creates a feeling of being out of control and having absolutely no power. God invites us to tell Him all about it. Tell the One who can do something about whatever it is that has you in such a state.

When you do what He asks, then He promises that you will have a peace that doesn't make sense. You won't know where it came from, and you won't know why it came. You just know it is there. Peace will come and put everything under control. First, though, you must make a move of sheer obedience and say, "I am going to give all of this anxiety to God."

Jan Silvious, *Big Girls Don't Whine*

It's All of Grace

*God . . . has reconciled us
to Himself through Jesus Christ.*

2 CORINTHIANS 5:18

When you received Christ by His Spirit,
He entered your heart and brought
forgiveness with Him (see Colossians 1:14).
He made you a whole new person inside and gave
you a whole new start (see 2 Corinthians 5:17).
He promised you that He would never abandon
you or throw you away (see John 6:37). You are
like a penny standing upright in the palm of his
nail-pierced hand. You may fall down, but you
can never fall out. The penny is so small, but the
hand of the One who loves you is so large. You
are His and He is yours. It's a sort of "exchanged
life." You get Christ and He gets you. To be sure,
He gets the raw end of the deal, but never mind,
that is all of grace!

Jill Briscoe, *Here Am I, Lord*

A MELODY RESTORED

Let all that you do be done with love.

1 CORINTHIANS 16:14

Who wants to be around someone who is critical? I don't see any raised hands out there. A critical spirit is constricting, cruel, and caustic. And being critical of others is as habit-forming as nicotine and caffeine and it stifles the music in our hearts. When I'm critical, that's often a warning that I'm too busy, too tired, and too self-absorbed.

So how can we have a melody restored?

Ask the Lord to give us a new song, a toe-tapping song of praise.

Practice praising others. Not empty words of someone trying too hard to impress but sincere words of truth so they fit into the hearer's heart.

Patsy Clairmont, *The Hat Box*

COME BOLDLY

Let us therefore come boldly to the throne of grace,
that we may obtain mercy
and find grace to help in time of need.

HEBREWS 4:16

Many years ago, we lost a baby girl. She was only fifteen days old. To this day, I feel a bond with women who have lost a baby. That woman knows my experience. I know her experience. I've been there. Scripture says Jesus has been there, too. He knows what you feel. If you are divorced and you know others in the Christian world who are divorced, you know the bond that grows when you talk to a woman whose husband left after twenty years of marriage. Through the sharing of the pain, the shock, and the rejection, you experience a bond. Scripture says Jesus did that, too. He has been where you and I have been, and because He's been there, He doesn't judge us in our weakness. He doesn't judge us when we're afraid. Instead, Scripture tells us to ". . . come boldly to the throne of grace, that we may obtain mercy and find grace to help in time of need" (Heb. 4:16).

Marilyn Meberg, *Overcoming Difficulties*

FINDING YOUR LIFE PASSION

*Every good gift and every perfect gift is from above,
and comes down from the Father of lights.*

JAMES 1:17

There is something that God is calling you to do. You know it. You've always known it. You may not know exactly what it is, or what shape it will ultimately take, but it is unique to you and it is why you were put here on this earth. I don't think this passion is just handed to us like a gift. I think it is revealed in us over time like an excavation. Everything extra gets chiseled away.

Finding your passion is the single most important ingredient for changing your world. It's like yeast in bread—without it you will have flat, hard dough. Uncovering God's purpose in your life and following it will lead you to the greatest satisfaction there is. When we work out of our God-given passion, we get tired, but not weary. We need rest, but not a change.

Nicole Johnson, *Fresh-Brewed Life*

Hold Tight to Hope

*You are my strong refuge. Let my mouth be filled with
Your praise and with Your glory all the day.*

PSALM 71:7–8

Fear is an emotion we've all encountered. Even
the bravest woman has felt the quite gnawing
of fear in her heart. It's wondering what might
happen. It's knowing things are out of our hands.
It's losing control. It's expecting the worst. It's
having the jitters. It's losing our appetite.
Queasiness. Sweating palms. Jangling nerves.
Furrowed brow. Trembling hands. Pounding heart.
Shortness of breath. Butterflies in the stomach.

When worry, anxiety, fretting, and fear
overwhelm our hearts and minds, we tend to
forget everything else. But God wants us to
remember one very important thing—Him. When
fears press in around you, cling to God. Hang
onto His promises for you. Hold
tight to hope. Trust God with
your very life, and your faith
will drive out the fears.

Christa Kinde,
Managing Your Moods

LIVING IN GOD'S ABUNDANCE

My God shall supply all your need
according to His riches in glory by Christ Jesus.

PHILIPPIANS 4:19

Sometimes we see our lives running counter to our desires, wishes, and prayers; we then assume God doesn't care. When these kinds of thoughts take over and undermine our faith, we have ceased to live in response to the abundance of God.

Living in response to the abundance of God is simply having the faith to rest in His provision and to believe in His individual care. Philippians 4:19 states, "My God shall supply all your need according to His riches in glory by Christ Jesus." That is a joy-producing scriptural reminder, because when our faith is strengthened our joy returns. When our joy returns, so does our smile.

Marilyn Meberg, *Choosing the Amusing*

The Prayer of Jabez

*"Oh, that You would bless me indeed,
and enlarge my territory, that Your hand would be
with me, and that You would keep me from evil,
that I may not cause pain!"*

1 CHRONICLES 4:10

As we read this brief prayer of Jabez, it becomes clear that this was not a man who longed to accumulate wealth for himself. He was instead a humble man desiring an enlarged sphere of influence that he might be more productive in carrying out the plans and purposes of the God in his life.

Here was a man whose heart was right toward his Maker and whose motive for asking touched the heart of God. The result? God granted him what he requested. Perhaps we should ask for the motive of Jabez before we ask for the blessing of Jabez.

Lana Bateman, *Women of Faith
Devotional Bible*

LAVISH GOD WITH PRAISE!

Sing to Him, sing psalms to Him;
talk of all His wondrous works!

1 CHRONICLES 16:9

Everyone enjoys being paid a compliment. Recently my husband, who doesn't care much for shopping, purchased a very nice shirt for himself. He didn't reveal his purchase until the following Sunday morning. He looked so handsome, and I didn't hesitate to tell him so. I was proud he had forged ahead through the department store to make such a nice purchase.

Our heavenly Father deserves the highest of compliments from us, His children. If you want to get God's full attention, praise Him. If your life is experiencing a deficit in the joy department, pay Him the most wonderful compliments your vocabulary will allow. As He showers you with lavish blessings, return thanks with extravagant praise. Your life will be much richer, fuller, and deeper.

Babbie Mason, *Women of Faith Devotional Bible*

At the Heart of Love

God is love. Whoever lives in love lives in God,
and God in him.

1 JOHN 4:16

Why do we easily forget about the gift we have in Jesus? A true confidante. A safe keeper of our secrets. A lover of our souls. There is an abundance of eternal treasure waiting to be discovered. There will always be mystery to God until we see Him face to face—but there is so much we could experience here and now. He longs to give us His jewels. Whether they are coming out of His mouth or displayed in the fabric of our lives, God Almighty wants to lavish us with all that He is. He always wants to let us know He loves us. And He will always find a way.

Kathy Troccoli, *Hope for a Woman's Heart*

WEDDING OF THE MILLENNIA

That He might present her to Himself a glorious church, not having spot or wrinkle or any such thing, but that she should be holy and without blemish.

EPHESIANS 5:27

We are being cleaned up, decked out, and ornamented for the wedding of the millennia! Jesus is preparing His people as a bride, making sure that we can be presented without spot or blemish. He has dressed us with garments of salvation and clothes of righteousness. We are like a bride, adorned with jewels (Isa. 61:10).

God is using His Word, His Spirit, Christ's blood, prayer, and all the rest to cleanse us, to robe us, to adorn us. It is part of His will for your life to have you undergo this sanctification. All this Bible study, prayer, and the living out of our faith is making the bride of Christ more and more beautiful. Your quiet times with God are better than beauty sleep, a trip to the hairdresser, and a day at the spa combined!

Christa Kinde, *Discovering God's Will for Your Life*

HALF-WAY HOME

*"Assuredly, I say to you, inasmuch as you did it to
one of the least of these My brethren, you did it to Me."*

MATTHEW 25:40

A friend sent me a card last year that said,
"When I was growing up in an East Texas
farming community, we had an old-fashioned
custom of 'walking a piece of the way home' with
our visitors. Guests who walked to our house were
accompanied halfway home after their visits. As a
little girl, I welcomed this extra time I could
spend with a cherished friend. Often these were
the most delightful moments of all. I'm a good
deal older now, and life's growing shorter. I am
nevertheless comforted that I have walked at least
part of the way home with a Friend—One who
walks with me always, everywhere."

Now imagine the joy of passing along that
blessing and walking someone else "half-way
home" to heaven. Wouldn't it be marvelous to
join that heavenly throng and have someone say,
"Because of YOU, I accepted Jesus' invitation to
spend eternity with Him"?

Barbara Johnson, *Leaking Laffs*

FORGIVE AND FIND RELIEF

Forgive us our debts, as we forgive our debtors.

MATTHEW 6:12

The person I needed to forgive the most was my father. When I was in the hospital, the doctors suggested I write him a letter. I thought, *That's stupid. My father's dead.* And that's what I told the doctors. "You'd be doing this for yourself," they said. "Write it with your left hand. You'll be less in control and you'll write what you really think and feel."

When I got out of the hospital. I sat down and wrote with my left hand. I was surprised at what poured out. I was angry at my dad for leaving me when I was a child and for my feeling responsible for my mother as a child.

I flew home to Scotland. My mom drove me the place where my dad was buried and left me alone. I read my dad the letter. The cemetery was quiet, and I felt a companionship with him that I had never known until then. Finally I forgave him for what he had no control of—and I forgave myself.

Sheila Walsh, *Life Is Tough but God Is Faithful*

An Amazing Exchange

*His divine power has given to us all things
that pertain to life and godliness.*

2 PETER 1:3

God seems to make a habit of redeeming the unworthy. Boy, am I grateful! We watch Him deliver the grumbling, complaining Hebrews out of their bitter slavery in Egypt; but lest we be too hard on them for their shortcomings, perhaps we had better take a look at our own call to freedom.

Before I met Christ when I was about thirty years old, I too had lived in terrible bondage. It had taken many years for me to come to the end of myself, but as I cried out to God asking Him to deliver me from my own self-destruction, He heard my prayer, became my Savior, and made me His child forever.

What an amazing exchange! We give him the filth of our lives, and He gives us liberty—the freedom to live and have our being in His love and forgiveness—while He makes His home in our hearts forever!

Lana Bateman, *Women of Faith Devotional Bible*

Overloaded by Life

*Rejoice in the LORD, you righteous, and give thanks at
the remembrance of His holy name.*

PSALM 97:12

Have you ever had one of those weeks? The
car keys are nowhere to be found. The in-
laws called out of the blue to let you know they're
dropping by on their way to Florida. You have
been out of dog food for two days. The kids have
come down with stomach flu. You get a flat tire.
You suddenly realize it was your sister's birthday
yesterday. There's a run in your pantyhose. The
baby must be teething again. Your son's piano
recital and your daughter's softball game are
scheduled for the same afternoon.

We really do have weeks when we feel
overloaded by life. Too much is happening, and our
sanity is under strain. Those are the times when it's
hard to rejoice. But those are the days when
joy is most needed!

Christa Kinde,
Women of Faith Devotional Bible

SERENDIPITOUS SURPRISES

*In Your hand it is to make great
and to give strength to all.*

1 CHRONICLES 29:12

Our journeys through life are regularly interrupted by detours from the intended course. On an average day, who can predict what might happen?

Life is full of serendipitous and surprising detours—not all of them easily accepted at the moment. We've all experienced life taking sudden turns. Sometimes we're carefree tourists and find ourselves in risky positions. Usually, we're minding our own business and, quite suddenly, we encounter the unexpected. These things happen in our lives every day, and we have the choice to either embrace our experience with a sense of trust or spend our energies fighting the inevitable. We can respond to challenges and opportunities with "Why not?" or we can react to reality with "Why me?" It is truly up to us how we'll encounter what is around the next bend.

Luci Swindoll, *I Married Adventure*

CREATED BY GOD

You formed my inward parts;
You covered me in my mother's womb.

PSALM 139:13

Just imagine how heaven grew silent and God's heart swelled with joy when —"Whaaaaaa!"— you arrived on earth to become, to be, to live! Another baby girl, created by Him was born! God is crazy about you! From the moment of your conception, He hovered over every week of your growth in the womb as you came to resemble more and more the person He designed you to be. He watched intently as you made your way into the world, screaming, writhing, and adjusting to earth's air. His complex little girl had been launched on her journey, which already was recorded in His book.

He knew your beginning. He knew the family that would shape you.

And yes, He even knew the struggles you would have along the way.

He knew them then and He knows them now. You can say without doubt, "How precious are your thoughts about me, O God."

Jan Silvious, *Big Girls Don't Whine*

THE WORLD IS WATCHING

*"By this all will know that you are My disciples,
if you have love for one another."*

JOHN 13:35

Unless we genuinely love each other, unless we truly care for each other, unless we are living in harmony, *the world will not believe.* There is so much dissension out there: quarreling, belittling, and misunderstanding. The world lives like this. The world lives without hope. We do much of the same. Why would anybody *without* Jesus want our life *with* Jesus if it looks the same? Believe me, they're watching. *We* watch! Why wouldn't they be watching!

Everybody wants the real deal. And when you show the real deal, the purity of love, it is hard to resist. There is no moving toward God without love. If we who bear His name do not love, Jesus tells us the world will dismiss *Him.*

Dee Brestin and Kathy Troccoli,
The Colors of His Love

GO STRAIGHT TO GOD

*The LORD spoke to Moses, saying, "I have heard the
complaints of the children of Israel."*

EXODUS 8:11–12

They had sand in their sandwiches, a
monotonous landscape, thirsty children, and
bickering families! I can't say I blame the children
of Israel for their complaints.

Most of the complaints of the people of God as
they tramped through the hard places of the desert
were quite understandable. There was no water and
there was no bread. You can't live without either, so
they had some good grounds for grumbling. The
mistake they made was to get after Moses and
Aaron instead of going straight to the Lord!

If only we would learn, at the start of our
spiritual journey, to take our complaint straight to
the complaint department. Notice where that is:
it is not the pastor's office or a helpful friend. It is
the Lord Himself we need to talk to. He is the
one who hears our grumbling, and He is the One
who can deal with it!

Jill Briscoe, *Here Am I, Lord*

Living Water

I will pour water on him who is thirsty,
and floods on the dry ground.

ISAIAH 44:3

I love plants. My home and office wouldn't seem quite the same without green things scattered about. Over the years I've had varying degrees of success with these plants, mainly because I sometimes forget to water them. Now, a plant can get along okay without the spritzing and dusting and fertilizing, but when you forget to water it, it just shrivels up and dies. The end. That's why most of my plants are philodendrons. They're virtually indestructible. They take my absentmindedness in stride.

Sometimes, I think my heart is like a philodendron, because I don't always take good care of it. It gets dusty with disuse, and I forget to feed it. Worse, I withhold it from God, and it suffers times of drought. But whenever I come to my senses and return to the Lord, my heart is soaked in living water and revives.

Christa Kinde, *Managing Your Moods*

THE PRINCE OF HEAVEN

*The Lord . . . is not willing that any should perish
but that all should come to repentance.*

2 PETER 3:9

The Prince of heaven is the truest prince who
ever lived—the Son of God. Sent to invite us
to enter the invisible kingdom. Sent to change
our lives forever by His great love. His desire is
that not one person should die without knowing
His love. He knows what our hearts long for. And
He smiles as He sees what happens to our hearts
when we are loved.

We don't have to wait any longer to be
found. We can stop hoping that someone else will
come and rescue us. He has already found us and
rescued us, and our hearts are set free to skip and
dance and respond to His love. It's what we were
made for. Love has redeemed our name.

Nicole Johnson, *Keeping a Princess Heart*

God's Unchanging Love

Trust in the LORD and do good;
dwell in the land, and feed on His faithfulness.

PSALM 37:3

Faithfulness is a wondrous attribute. It's all about reliability, steadiness, firmness, and supportiveness. Our God holds steady when we're standing tall and when we take a foolish fall. We can be in our worst mood or on our Sunday-best behavior; yet He remains trustworthy.

I used to believe God loved me as long as I behaved. Oh, I don't think I ever verbalized that as my belief, but I certainly behaved as though it were true. Problem was I couldn't behave. Then one day, like a lantern being lit in a cave, it came to me that in the midst of my worst behavior Christ wooed me into His love. And if He could love me as raucous as I was then, I could trust Him to be faithful and to love me through till glory. His acceptance of us isn't based on our behavior but on His unchanging love.

Patsy Clairmont, *The Shoe Box*

A God of Help and Hope

Lord, it is nothing for You to help,
whether with many or with those who have no power.

2 CHRONICLES 14:11

When I found myself in the midst of tragic circumstances and no finances, fear began to overwhelm me. What about my home? I wasn't emotionally ready to leave it. Could I dare hope that God would meet my need?

A few days later a young gentleman came to me for lay counseling. When we finished our time together, he wrote a check and put it on the coffee table, asking me not to look at it until he was gone. When I turned that check over, I fell to my knees in tears. It was $11,000—exactly the amount needed to make house payments for a whole year!

Though God doesn't answer all of our prayers in the same way, He moves on even the smallest amount of faith. He is ever proving to us that He can be trusted and we can place all of our faith and hope in Him.

Lana Bateman,
Women of Faith Devotional Bible

ENORMOUS RELIEF

*"In Your hand is there not power and might,
so that no one is able to withstand You?"*

2 CHRONICLES 20:6

What do you do when you find yourself up against overwhelming odds? Jehoshaphat was king of Judah when not one, but three armies gathered outside the city gates. Jehoshaphat gathered everyone together and they cried out to God. He grounded his plea on the sovereign power of God and His promises. That God had chosen them as His people and promised them the land was reason enough to trust Him—even with the enemy at the gates.

God rules over all the kingdoms of the earth. No power, no rule and authority, can surmount His. "I, the LORD, have called You in righteousness, and will hold your hand; I will keep You," Isaiah declares (Isa. 42:6). What an enormous relief to trust a God who rules the universe—and who also promises to hold us personally by the hand and watch over us.

Paula Rinehart, *Women of Faith Devotional Bible*

You Are the Church

*All the people . . . they praised the LORD, because the
foundation of the house of the LORD was laid.*

EZRA 3:11

Solomon's temple had been destroyed 66 years
before the foundation of the new temple was
laid. Haggai 2:1-5 tells us that the prophet encouraged
the people not to be disappointed in the outward
appearance of the building, but to be strong and
work, for the Lord Almighty was with them.

The shouts of the new generation, who were
just delighted to have any sort of a temple, drowned
out the sobs of the elderly who remembered the
glory days. Worship was once more at the center of
the life of God's people and, after all, that was what
really mattered.

Some of the most meaningful experiences of
my spiritual life have been in churches with no
walls, no ceilings, no seats, and no sound systems.
This is not to say facilities do not facilitate
ministry, but the church, as my husband loves to
say, is something you are, not somewhere you go.

Jill P. Briscoe, *Women of Faith Devotional Bible*

WHEN WE SEEK HIM

*The hand of our God is upon
all those for good who seek Him.*

EZRA 8:22

It's easy to say God is in control during mountaintop experiences, but other times we question God's sovereignty.

When faced with tragedies, such as terrorist attacks, the loss of a loved one, a job demotion, an unfaithful mate, or a fatal diagnosis, it's easy to doubt that God is in control. But, regardless of the situation, it is always our responsibility to humble ourselves through fasting and prayer and to seek God to show us the way.

"Thank you, God, that when we are faithful to seek You, You are faithful to answer. You are always in control!"

Sara Trollinger, *Women of Faith Devotional Bible*

The Faithful Few

He who calls you is faithful, who also will do it.

1 THESSALONIANS 5:24

Do you ever wonder how the saints who have gone before feel about having their lives recorded in the Bible? At first you might think, *Wow! I'd love that!* People would read about you for centuries after you were gone. Mothers would name their babies after you. You'd have your own little figure on those flannel-graph boards. But then it dawns on you: You won't get to approve the final manuscript, and God might include some pretty embarrassing things in your life story.

Just look at the "faithful" few. Eve was a blame-shifter. Abraham told lies to protect himself. Sarah was jealous of a younger woman. Rebekah played favorites with her children. Peter tended to speak before thinking. Martha let busyness distract her from the Lord. They weren't so very different from us after all. It is only by God's grace that any of us are saved.

Christa Kinde, *Women of Faith Devotional Bible*

May

*God means
for us to experience joy.*

LET GOD FIX IT

*Let your ear be attentive and Your eyes open,
that You may hear the prayer of Your servant.*

NEHEMIAH 1:6

Have you ever come to the end of yourself and recognized there is a God, and you are not Him? Seems to me that's where Nehemiah found himself as he "sat down and wept, and mourned for many days" (Neh. 1:4). He needed to know that not only was there a God, but there was a God who was totally in control of his world.

Nehemiah had received bad news about his people. They were in great distress, and the city he loved was in ruins. Instead of rushing to fix the situation, he turned to the Sovereign God who is all-knowing and all-powerful.

In Nehemiah there is a picture of what you can do when your world crumbles. Instead of rushing to intervene in the problem, turn to the only One who can fix it.

Jan Silvious, *Women of Faith
Devotional Bible*

REAL FRIENDSHIP

*"Which of these three do you think was neighbor
to him who fell among the thieves?"
And he said, "He who showed mercy on him."*

MATTHEW 10:36–37

Jesus told the story of the good Samaritan in
answer to the lawyer's question, "Who is my
neighbor?" This simple story surely shows that we
may find ourselves in situations where we need
compassion, but we might not always get it.
Those whom we think will offer it do not, and
when compassion does appear, it comes from
unlikely neighbors, indeed.

Each one of us needs to have friends who will
care for us, even when we don't deserve to be cared
for. Real friendship means that even when someone
falls and makes mistakes, we are still there for
them. Our relationships are not up for negotiation.
One of the secrets to keeping on when life is
tough is to have friends who know God and love
Him. Then they can reach out to know and love
you as well.

Sheila Walsh, *Life Is Tough but God Is Faithful*

CATCH THE JOY!

The joy of the LORD is your strength.

NEHEMIAH 8:10

The most important meaning of the word *joy* for me has to do with what Nehemiah told the children of Israel when they were lamenting about the sins of their fathers. Nehemiah told them to stop crying and feeling sorry for themselves for things they could not change. "Dry your eyes," he said. "Have a party. The future belongs to you. For the joy of the Lord is your strength."

Joy is that emotion that tickles your tickle box or makes your eyes bright and gleaming. Joy springs assurance in your being when your circumstances look bleak. Joy is the excitement of Jesus swelling up in your heart when there is no earthly reason to be excited. Joy is the confirmation in your soul that, whatever happens in life, Jesus is right beside you—giving you the strength you need for the journey. So when you begin to fret and cry, catch the joy!

Thelma Wells, *Women of Faith Devotional Bible*

SCARLET ASSURANCE

You were not redeemed with corruptible things,
. . . but with the precious blood of Christ.

1 PETER 1:18–19

Joy in Christ. I call it "a scarlet assurance." Moses could turn his fear to joy after he put the scarlet blood above the lintel and doorpost of the Jewish homes so the destroyer would not kill their firstborn.

When I was a single mom, I encountered some grave, rebellious days with one of my children. As I prayed about these challenges, I pictured the roof of our house painted scarlet red. I imagined God looking down and pouring out His blessings and keeping curses away from all the scarlet roofs He found. When I gave my needs back to Him, life no longer seemed so overwhelming.

So how can you and I be joyful, even when tough times surround us? Jesus spilled His scarlet blood on Calvary's cross so that you and I can have not only eternal life, but also abundant life. That's reason to be joyful!

Lynda Hunter-Bjorklund,
Women of Faith Devotional Bible

MAY 5

God Listens, God Cares

Now this is the confidence that we have in Him, that
if we ask anything according to His will, He hears us.

1 JOHN 5:14

Prayer is the key to accessing the power of the
Holy Spirit within you. You open your
mouth and use your words. You open your heart
and reveal your concern. You unite with the Spirit
in the knowledge He will answer you. In its most
simplified form, that is prayer. Prayer is talking
to God.

The moment we begin talking to God and
making our needs known, we are accessing the
power of the Spirit. As the psalmist wrote,
"When I pray, you answer me." God hears us
and begins immediately to help us with the
concerns in our lives.

That's why we talk to God about everything.
He listens, He cares, and He works for us. That
praying accesses the Spirit power within us.

Marilyn Meberg, *Assurance for a Lifetime*

FRESH-BREWED LIFE

*God has sent His only begotten Son into the world,
that we might live through Him.*

1 JOHN 4:9

Surrendering to God is the key that unlocks
the door to the life you want. A bigger
spiritual "to do" list or a calendar full of church
activities will not change our lives. When we give
ourselves to God—mind, body, soul, and spirit—
He changes us. We cannot change ourselves.
We don't have enough spiritual stamina to change
ourselves, let alone another person or the world.
But when the walls come down and He has access
to the deepest parts of who we are, His love
courses through us in a cleansing, holy way.
And we are different because of it. Stronger, richer.
As different as instant coffee is from fresh-brewed.
We become a full cup of steaming inviting life.

Nicole Johnson, *Fresh-Brewed Life*

GLADNESS, JOY, AND HONOR

The Jews had light and gladness, joy and honor.

ESTHER 8:15

If you want your life to be marked with gladness, joy, and honor, you have to have "light." Jesus said, "I am the light of the world" (John 8:12). So when Jesus is in your life, you see things differently because you have light.

You see that you are never alone.

You see that He gives you everything you need to get through this day.

You see that He is a Friend who sticks closer to you than any blood relative.

You see that He is your comfort when you desperately need to know someone cares.

And when the awareness of who Jesus is to you really dawns in your life, you are filled with gladness, joy, and honor! What a deal!

Jan Silvious, *Women of Faith Devotional Bible*

GOD'S STRENGTH IS OURS

He gives power to the weak,
and to those who have no might He increases strength.

ISAIAH 40:29

It's silly to pretend we're always skipping along
under blue skies with a happy heart. There are
days when we just don't feel like skipping. There are
days when the skies are not blue, but a nondescript
shade of beige. We feel blah. Lackluster. Uninspired.
Disinterested. We just don't care. Those are the
days when we're not in the mood for anything.
We don't feel like smiling. We don't feel like talking.
We don't feel like working. We don't feel like
cooking. And we certainly don't feel like putting
any effort into being pleasant. Often, we'd really
rather everyone just go away.

Unfortunately, we cannot pause life just because
we're not in the mood for it. A woman's got to do
what a woman's got to do, whether she feels like it or
not. Those are times when we have to reach right
down into that heart of ours and find enough
strength from the Lord to make it through the next
day, the next hour, or even the next minute.

Christa Kinde, *Managing Your Moods*

ROLL INTO GOD'S GRACE

*Commit your works to the LORD,
and your thoughts will be established.*

PROVERBS 16:3

I had such a sense that this verse was indeed a special word from God to my heart that I began a word study of the verse. The word *commit* in the context of this verse is very interesting. The Hebrew word is *galal*. It means, "To roll; roll away."

The word *galal* is used often to describe the way a camel gets rid of its burden. It is a two-step process. First, it kneels down, and then it rolls to the left and the load falls off it's back. The picture for us is a beautiful one. We are invited to kneel before God but encouraged not to stop there. We are called to roll over and let the burden fall off our backs. We are called to roll every burden, every concern for the future, onto the Lord, sure that He will accept that responsibility and will bless us. *Whatever you are facing right now, kneel before God and roll into His grace.* He wants to carry your burden. You don't have to carry it anymore.

Sheila Walsh, *The Heartache No One Sees*

FILLED WITH LAUGHING

He will yet fill your mouth with laughing,
and your lips with rejoicing.

JOB 8:21

Job lost everything that was dear and valuable to him—his livestock, his possessions, his servants, his family, and even his health. Before his miserable ordeal ended, he had only one thing left: his questioning but enduring faith that God was still on the throne, still in control.

Job's story is hard for most of us to read. We wince and shudder as we read of the heartbreaking torments that beset him. Yet, ironically, within the story of Job's agony I find an unshakable promise of joy. It comes in a set of platitudes spoken by Job's friend Bildad, meant to encourage Job. Now, to tell the truth, in some of their counseling Job's friends were about as helpful as fleas on a dog, but this remark by Bildad was right on the money. Bildad told the suffering Job, "He will yet fill your mouth with laughing, and your lips with rejoicing" (Job 8:21).

Barbara Johnson, *Women of Faith Devotional Bible*

LOVE AND MARRIAGE

Now abide faith, hope, love, these three;
but the greatest of these is love.

1 CORINTHIANS 13:13

When my three children were talking about getting married, one thing I told each of them to remember was, "If there's something about your prospective spouse that you can't stand now, multiply that by one thousand times, and that's how bad it's going to feel after you are married. Don't get married thinking you will mold your spouse into your image. It won't work! You can't change anybody. I don't care how good he looks to you now, you'll wake up one morning, look at him, and think, *What in the world have I done? I can't stand him today!* That doesn't mean you don't love him. It means that the things you don't like about him are really getting on your nerves and you can't do a thing about it. So be careful about choosing a spouse. If God didn't put you together, don't you get together."

Thelma Wells, *Girl, Have I Got Good News for You*

BE NOBODY BUT YOU

I will give thanks to You,
for I am fearfully and wonderfully made.

PSALM 139:14

Sometimes it is tough to be me because I don't like me. I'm disappointed in me. I'm embarrassed at the way I look, or I'm not being understood and affirmed by somebody I want to love me. Clearly, without doubt, there is nothing wrong with seeking to change in ourselves what is able to be changed (I am a strong advocate of that). But the essence of who we are—our age, our sex, our looks, our past, our shortcomings, our broken promises to ourselves, our unfulfilled dreams—we must learn to live with and to accept for what it is. We must seek to walk in God's light and in His counsel, realizing that contentment, acceptance, love, compassion, vulnerability, and charm are the byproducts of an intimate relationship with Him, not the results of conforming to the mandates and demands of an insatiable world.

Luci Swindoll,
You Bring the Confetti God Brings the Joy

FINDING SPIRITUAL WATER

*I will pour water on him who is thirsty,
and floods on the dry ground.*

ISAIAH 44:3

Our home in Wisconsin is located in a beautiful country district, and for this reason we are dependent on a well for water. One day, like the woman at the well, I found myself seeking. Our well was dry, and I had to telephone the local well diggers. They told me how much per foot it would cost to drill deep enough to find water, but they couldn't tell me how deep that would be because they didn't know. They could say only that it would be a costly enterprise. It was. But not nearly as costly an enterprise as finding spiritual water for a dying spirit and soul! That enterprise cost the Son of God His life on the cross.

Jill Briscoe, *Here Am I, Lord*

LAUGHING EACH DAY

A merry heart does good, like medicine.

PROVERBS 17:22

Laugh therapist Bob Basso, whom I heard at a stress-reduction conference, stated that 52 percent of us would die from stress or stress-related illnesses in the next thirty years. His remedy: Have fun when you can and laugh even when you can't. The alternative is to experience an inevitable eroding of health.

God has prescribed a joyful heart as good medicine and scientists are now saying our body's natural painkillers are released when we laugh.

The oft-repeated scriptural imperative "rejoice" takes on new significance as we realize what happens physiologically when we do rejoice. God means for us to experience joy. It is not His intent that we suffer from ulcers, migraine headaches, and other stress-related illnesses. The Scriptures remind us that "He who is of a merry heart has a continual feast"(Prov. 15:15).

Marilyn Meberg, *Choosing the Amusing*

GOD'S GOAL

*I press on, that I may lay hold of that
for which Christ Jesus has also laid hold of me.*

PHILIPPIANS 3:12

God's goal is not necessarily to make us happy. God's goal is to make us His.

There are thousands of times when we'll ask God what He is doing to us. We must be more concerned with what He wants to do in us. I am talking about conforming us into the image of Christ. And only the Lord knows what it will take to conform us into the image of His son.

John Newton said: "Trials are medicines which our gracious and wise physician prescribes because we need them; and he proportions the frequency and weight of them to what the case requires. Let us trust in His skill and thank Him for His prescription."

Kathy Troccoli,
Hope for a Woman's Heart

"WHATEVER, LORD!"

"Though He slay me, yet will I trust Him."

JOB 13:15

Two important principles have helped me survive the trials of life with joy in my heart.

First, remember that we are pilgrims here, not settlers. Whatever we're enduring in this life is temporary. As Christians we have mansions waiting for us in heaven; that means our final exit here will be our grandest entrance there! If you keep your focus on that heavenly promise, then you'll know that, no matter what life throws at you, you and God can handle it.

Second, instead of whining, "Why me?" learn to say, "Whatever, Lord!" God is in control. Nothing comes into our lives without passing through His filter. He has a plan to bring us through our earthly existence to join Him in a glorious eternity. So vow to have the same faith Job had and say, in the midst of your troubles, "Though He slay me, yet will I trust Him."

Barbara Johnson, *Women of Faith Devotional Bible*

GIVE UP GRUMBLING

It is better to dwell in a corner of a housetop,
than in a house shared with a contentious woman.

PROVERBS 25:24

I have always been amazed at the children of Israel. Have you ever seen such an ungrateful lot? God frees them from their chains, drowns their pursuers, shades them with a cloud by day, provides them with a nightlight at night, brings forth water in the midst of the desert, gives them bread from heaven itself, talks one-on-one with their leader, and promises them beautiful new homes in a land that will be all theirs. What slave would have dreamed so much? But they are not thankful. Worse, they complain!

I wonder what would have happened if the Israelites had considered their circumstances with a brighter eye, and simply said, "Thank you, Lord." Let's beware ourselves that we don't fall into the trap of murmuring! God's will for our lives doesn't include griping and grumbling. We are called to an attitude of gratitude!

Christa Kinde, *Discovering God's Will for Your Life*

GOD'S BOUNDLESS LOVE

Eye has not seen, nor ear heard,
nor have entered into the heart of man the things which
God has prepared for those who love Him.

1 CORINTHIANS 2:9

God has the absolute right to do anything He pleases. That's a frightening thought, isn't it? We like to think of ourselves as in control; sometimes we even like to think that we are controlling God by adhering to a list of spiritual dos and don'ts.

But the Lord to whom we have entrusted our lives has the right and authority to take our health, our property, even our loved ones. The good news is that, no matter what, we can trust that His acts are motivated by His boundless love for us.

Angela Elwell Hunt, *Women of Faith Devotional Bible*

The Last Laugh Is Ours!

*My God shall supply all your need
according to His riches in glory in Christ Jesus.*

PHILIPPIANS 4:19

Living in response to the abundance of God is simply having the faith to rest in His provision and to believe in His individual caring. The familiar Philippians 4:19 passage states, "My God shall supply all your need according to His riches in glory in Christ Jesus." These are joy-producing scriptural reminders. They can strengthen our faith because when our faith is strengthened, our joy returns. When our joy returns, so does our smile. That smile then becomes a positive witness to the reality of our faith.

We, as believers in Christ, who conquered death, have the last laugh. As we walk through this life, we encounter pain, we encounter heartache, and we encounter sorrow. But at the end of it all, we encounter God! The last laugh is ours!

Marilyn Meberg,
Choosing the Amusing

GOD DELIGHTS IN HUMILITY

If My people, who are called by My name,
will humble themselves and pray . . .
then will I hear from heaven and
will forgive their sin and will heal their land.

2 CHRONICLES 7:14

Because humility is the opposite of pride, it is no surprise that our Lord would make it a prerequisite to prayer, for God hates pride. One verse of Scripture that speaks powerfully regarding the issue of prayer and humility is: *"Then [the angel] said to me, Do not by afraid, Daniel, for from the first day that you set your heart on understanding . . . and on humbling yourself before your God, your words were heard, and I have come in response to your words"* (Dan. 10:12, NAS). In this passage God teaches us two principles of prayer. The first is that answered prayer often comes as a result of our desire to understand, and the second is the need for our willingness to humble ourselves before God.

Lana Bateman, *The Heart of Prayer*

TEARS IN A BOTTLE

You number my wanderings;
put my tears into Your bottle;
are they not in Your book?

PSALM 56:8

Jesus holds my tears in a bottle. Our tears. Not one of them falls to the ground without His hands intervening to save them.

Haven't we often thought we were alone in our grief? That God had forgotten us? "He's God and He can do something!" we cry. Meanwhile, He is always "doing something." Even when He is seemingly doing nothing, He is doing something. A behind-the-scenes Director who is orchestrating a Divine story. There is always a purpose. Always a plan. He feels deeply. He is moved greatly. He lets us bury our heads in His chest, and as He wipes our tears He wipes His own.

Kathy Troccoli, *Hope for a Woman's Heart*

SAFE IN THE STORM

I will both lie down in peace, and sleep;
for You alone, O LORD, make me dwell in safety.

PSALM 4:8

In north Georgia where my family and I live,
the landscape displays tall Georgia pine trees.
While the stately tree is beautiful, during even the
mildest storm our yards and streets are littered
with tree limbs. The landscape in south Georgia is
different, though. Along the balmy coast stands
the stately palm tree. This tree is not the least bit
moved by the threat of strong winds. You see, the
palm tree's trunk and deep root system allow it to
bend, but not break. It possesses great resistance
and resilience, even in the fiercest storm.

When the Word of God is in you, you don't
have to worry about life's storms. You can even lie
down at night and rest peacefully, knowing that
God is in control. Your heavenly Father will be up
all night so you, my friend, might as well get
some sleep.

Babbie Mason, *Women of Faith Devotional Bible*

FULLNESS OF JOY

In Your presence is fullness of joy;
at Your right hand are pleasure forevermore.

PSALM 16:11

What secret do believers filled with joy know? They practice the presence of God. Remember the euphoria you had as a new believer? How amazed you were to discover that the God who made the universe loved you and might intervene personally in your day! You were on the right track then, but so often as time passes we lose that sense of anticipation, we lose the glow.

Run after God the way you did when you first fell in love. Wake up talking to Him, thanking Him for the hot shower, the fragrance of coffee. Ask Him for direction for your day. Expect Him to speak to you from His Word. Watch for Him in the people who cross your path—yes, even in the interruptions. Talk with Him in the night. Set the Lord always before you, and He will fill you with joy and with pleasures forevermore.

Dee Brestin, *Women of Faith Devotional Bible*

GOODWILL AND GRACE

*Let the words of my mouth and the
meditation of my heart be acceptable in Your sight,
O LORD, my strength and my Redeemer.*

PSALM 19:14

I love words! In the night they accumulate inside of me, and then at daybreak I split open like an overripe watermelon spewing words like seeds. It is said that women have more words and a greater need to speak them than men. Yet I've met many sedate women; in fact, I collect quiet friends for obvious reasons.

So imagine when I stumbled on Psalm 19:14 and realized the words I speak should be acceptable to the Lord. Acceptable? In the Hebrew *acceptable* means "full of favor, kindness, goodwill, and grace." Hmm . . . that edited my utterances dramatically. I'd been given to bouts of nitpicking, sporadic sessions of whining, and spouts of vanity. Conversationally, I was at least three quarts low on grace.

With the Lord's help, I have given up my endless verbiage (generally) and weigh my words more carefully (usually).

Patsy Clairmont, *Women of Faith Devotional Bible*

No Need to Be Afraid

God has not given us a spirit of fear,
but of power and of love and of a sound mind.

2 TIMOTHY 1:7

Bryna, my two-year-old granddaughter, was happily eating her pizza. Everything was fine as long as the restaurant's huge, mechanical mascot was staying its distance and standing in place. But when the animated mascot started toward her table, she slid under the table hiding from this bigger-than-life, walking creature. She disappeared quickly! When her other grandmother and aunt saw her under the table, they asked what she was doing. Bryna's reply was, "I got to get outta here. I got to go!"

That's the way it seems when the circumstances of life look dangerously threatening. We want to get under the table or exit quickly. God's plans for us are different. He wants us to know that the "creatures" of our lives do not cause the casualties. It's the way we choose to deal with them.

Thelma Wells, *Women of Faith Devotional Bible*

An Attitude of Gratitude

In everything give thanks;
for this is the will of God in Christ Jesus for you.

1 THESSALONIANS 5:18

In the small, Midwestern town where I grew up, there were a lot of little catch phrases people used. Some make me smile when I think of them, like "you betcha" and "ufda." Others can be mildly frustrating, like "whatever," or "it could be worse." But my favorite old-timer phrase is a real staple—"Can't complain."

What a useful phrase! For instance, how do you respond to the usual "Hi, how are you?" Do you say "good," "fine," "hanging in there," "just great," "couldn't be better," or "swell"? Why not try "can't complain" for a while? If you start all your conversations with this little phrase, you'll be reminded to take your own advice, and not complain! It'll give your attitude of gratitude a little nudge in the right direction.

Christa Kinde,
Cultivating Contentment

BE STILL AND KNOW GOD

Lead me in Your truth and teach me, for You are
the God of my salvation; on You I wait all the day.

PSALM 25:5

Truth be known, I don't wait well. I get antsy. Hurry is my theme song. I strum my fingers on tabletops, and I don't like waiting rooms. In fact, it is a discipline for me to sit through dinner. I squirm a lot. When I fly I take a carry-on the size of a steamer trunk, filled with items to entertain myself. So, with this confession, you can imagine what a learning experience it has been for me to "wait all the day" on the Lord.

I want to know the Lord's ways; I want Him to teach me His paths and lead me in His truth, but I want it to happen *now.* The verse, "Be still and know that I am God" (Ps. 46:10), was definitely written for folks wired like me. That's one thing about God's Word: It will expose weaknesses, flaws, inconsistencies, and motives for the purpose of resolve. I guess that is why the psalmist exclaims, "The entrance of Your words gives light" (Ps. 119:130).

Patsy Clairmont, *Women of Faith Devotional Bible*

HOPE

I will always have hope.

PSALM 71:14

The hope of heaven sustains us in our earthly struggles and pushes us closer to God. As Joni Eareckson Tada said, "Suffering hurries the heart homeward." For Christians, home is heaven! That's our eternal home as well as our endearing hope, a hope someone defined as

He
Offers
Peace
Eternal.

The hope of heaven, the knowledge that we'll someday enjoy "peace eternal," means we can face *anything* here on earth as long as we focus on the joy that's waiting on us in heaven. We cling to this hope as a constant reminder in good times and in bad. As the psalmist wrote, "I will always have hope."

Barbara Johnson,
Leaking Laffs

FROM DARKNESS TO LIGHT

Oh, how I love Your law!
It is my meditation all the day.

PSALM 119:97

What is it about the Bible that catches us off guard? That reaches into the depths of our souls and little by little begins to straighten us out? It digs up our arrogance and pride and enables us to forgive and forget. It creates spaces for understanding that we would not have thought possible, much less tolerated. Nothing of humankind can do that for us. Only God's Spirit has the ability to reach that deep into life. The Word of God is powerful enough to change darkness to light and dissatisfaction to joy.

Luci Swindoll, *I Married Adventure*

ONE THING MATTERS

*"Mary has chosen that good part,
which will not be taken away from her."*

LUKE 10:38

Martha . . . welcomed Jesus to her home and went about with great fanfare putting a meal on the table. She was bustling about when it occurred to her that Mary was sitting around while there was work to be done. Martha spoke with Jesus about this breach of good behavior. Unruffled by her annoyance, Jesus went to the heart of the whole problem, and it wasn't Mary. It was what Martha was thinking. When He said, "Martha, Martha, you are worried and troubled about many things," He was really saying something much deeper than, "I'm so sorry you're in a tizzy over the matzo balls." He was saying, "Martha, you have a lot of things going on in your mind that are distracting you from the most important thing, which Mary has chosen."

What had Mary found? She had discovered the sweet truth that in the grand scheme of things, only one thing really matters: a relationship with Jesus.

Jan Silvious, *Big Girls Don't Whine*

A FEELING OF JOY

*Our fellowship is with the Father
and with His Son Jesus Christ. And these things
we write to you that your joy may be full.*

1 JOHN 1:3–4

We know vacations lift our spirits, that the first daffodils pushing up through the frozen earth gladden our hearts, but have we ever experienced a continuous *full* feeling of joy? Life is hard and some of us just barely get glimpses of happiness. So many holes in our hearts need to be filled. We long for hope, we long for peace, we long to belong, and we long to feel at home.

Jesus tells us that in this world we will have trouble, and we do. Yet John says fellowship with the Father and with the Son will make our joy complete. So if it does not mean freedom from trouble, what does it mean? Living in *complete joy* requires living in *complete confidence* in God. Each day can have a little more peace than yesterday, last month, or even a year ago, because though we still have sorrow, our joy is inextinguishable when we completely trust the heart of God.

Dee Brestin and Kathy Troccoli, *The Colors of His Love*

June

Happiness depends on something.

Joy depends on Someone.

GOD FULFILLS HIS PURPOSES

*All Your works shall praise You,
O LORD, and Your saints shall bless You.*

PSALM 145:10

God is working on two fronts all the time. As He works to transform society, He works to transform the transformers!

Here's how it works. God transports us to a situation. There is no such thing as happenstance in the life of a child of God. His intent is to use fallible people to give out His infallible truth to a world living in error. He wants to use weak people who love and obey Him to transform the society to which they have been transported. Then, as we tell others, our own lives are changed in the process.

It is quite exciting to realize we live in the right country at the right time for the right reason. Even if the world we were born into, moved to, or traveled to of our own free will is in turmoil. There are three important words on God's mind as He works His will in our world: location, location, location! He plants us where He will in order to fulfill His purposes.

Jill Briscoe, *Here Am I, Lord*

CONSTANT GRACE

God is able to make all grace abound toward you, that you . . . may have an abundance for every good work.

2 CORINTHIANS 9:8

We're still working so hard to make God love us, and life is tough and we wonder what we've done wrong. Our battered egos want to believe that something about us can earn or lose the love of God. Nothing about us can do this.

We are right to want to do better. God is worth that—and much more. But the harsh reality of life this side of Eden is that we are powerless to do so without the faithfulness and love of God. Look at Peter. Privileged to walk side by side with Jesus day after day. Saw the miracles. Saw Lazarus raised from the dead. But when hard confrontation came, he said he'd never met Jesus.

Human history is an ongoing story of stumbling men and women and the constant grace and mercy of God. It's all about Him, never about us.

Sheila Walsh, *Life Is Tough but God Is Faithful*

STEADFAST STEPS

*He has put a new song in my mouth—
praise to our God.*

PSALM 40:3

Stop and think about the last time you were
in the pits. What helped you climb out?
A person? A kindness? A medication? A book?
A break? Or perhaps a Scripture?

One of my favorite pit verses is Psalm
40:2–3. It is chock-full of victory and hope. "He
also brought me up out of a horrible pit, out of
the miry clay, and set my feet upon a rock, and
established my steps. He has put a new song in
my mouth—praise to our God."

David had known the darkness of
disappointment, depression, and despair; yet he
climbed out of those pits with God's help. I love
the word pictures of the rock-solid place to stand,
the steadfast steps, and a new
song—all because of God's
unchanging ways.

Patsy Clairmont, *The Hat Box*

FORGIVENESS FOR YOU

*If you forgive men their trespasses, your heavenly
Father will also forgive you.*

MATTHEW 6:14

I believe forgiveness is more for you than for the other person. More often than not, the person you are not forgiving is unconcerned about or unaware of your feelings. Who have you hurt by not forgiving? Yourself!

An older preacher once said to me: "You are not responsible for how people treat you. You are only responsible for your response to them." So true! When you fail to forgive anybody of anything, you allow him to determine the quality of your life. He controls you whether you want to admit it or not. The only sensible, Christian thing to do is to put the situation in the hands of the Lord and let Him wash you with the water of forgiveness. Forgiveness is work. But it's worth the doing. When you really forgive, the snake still bites, but the poison doesn't penetrate.

Thelma Wells, *Girl, Have I Got Good News for You*

THE SUNSHINE OF LIFE

A man who has friends must himself be friendly,
but there is a friend who sticks closer than a brother.

PROVERBS 18:24

A poet once described friends as "the sunshine of life." I myself have found that the day is certainly much brighter when I'm sharing it with my friends. Enjoying fellowship is one of life's sweetest blessings and joys. What would we do without people and the many shadings of companionship and camaraderie? We need friends in our lives, friends with whom we not only discuss "deep" issues and confide our secrets, fears, or sorrows, but with whom we can laugh, play, and even cry. The best times in life are made a thousand times better when shared with a dear friend.

Camaraderie is definitely a part of friendship, and camaraderie itself can often produce friendships, too. When we reach out to others, they reach out to us. It's a two-way street, a street practically lined with balloons and streamers in celebration of the unique bonds of friendship.

Luci Swindoll, *You Bring the Confetti*

LIFE IN CHRIST

He will rejoice over you with gladness, He will quiet you with his love, He will rejoice over you with singing.

ZEPHANIAH 3:17

Life is an open invitation to adventure for all. It's not only for the brave, but for the timid-hearted as well. It's a call to the Tomboy and the Tinkerbell. The great adventure of life in Christ is possible not because the world is "safe," but because our Father God is watching over us. We will never take a trip without Him. We will never be left behind. We will never put our head down on a pillow at night and be alone. Our God is with us, where He belongs. He even sings over us—a love song so beautiful we will never want Him to stop when we hear it with our hearts. Because of the security of His perfect love, we can be honest about where we are and dream of where we would like to go. Our fears and hopes are in our Father's safekeeping.

Sheila Walsh, *The Great Adventure*

CHOOSING TO BELIEVE

He has made everything beautiful in its time.

ECCLESIASTES 3:11

Every day we are at the mercy of Jesus. Every day we choose to believe or not to believe. There must be some sort of foundation to build our beliefs upon in order to move forward in our faith. There must be some anchor we throw out to know we will not be moved. There has to be. Without it, every hour and every emotion that passes will toss us like the wind. That anchor must be Jesus.

We so often encounter a people that have no concept of reality or of the truth of the gospel. They opt for psychics, stones, and candles because there is no cost. Nothing is required of them there. There is no bottom line to their actions or their morals without the absolute truths of God. It is very easy these days to create our own reality and adhere to it. Jesus challenges us to His reality.

Kathy Troccoli,
Hope for a Woman's Heart

Be Honest with Yourself

*We are hard-pressed on every side,
yet not crushed; we are perplexed, but not in despair.*

2 CORINTHIANS 4:8

Many people have secret places where they hide and lick their wounds. They choose to live a life of denial and doubt rather than be honest with themselves. Sometimes they are unaware of what they're hiding, or why.

For so many of us, it takes years to come face-to-face with the fears that lurk in our past. We bury them so deeply because we are convinced that if they were released they would overwhelm us. We don't allow ourselves to think about them even for a moment, but their long shadows cast a dark cloud over our minds nonetheless.

The Greek word for *salvation* means "to save, to heal, to make complete." That is what happens at the cross. The Father is committed to shining His light into the darkest corners where fear and sorrow lurk and bringing peace.

Sheila Walsh, *Life Is Tough but God Is Faithful*

The Strength of the Spirit

*But you shall receive power
when the Holy Spirit has come upon you.*

ACTS 1:8

Remember the Old Testament character Samson? When he and his parents were walking to a neighboring village, Samson was suddenly attacked by a young lion. He had an immediate need of "overcoming power," and he got it. "At that moment the Spirit of the LORD powerfully took control of him, and he ripped the lion's jaw apart with his bare hands" (Judges 14:6, NLT).

There are some addictions and other unhealthy habits that can be as life threatening as an unexpected lion attack. When they hit, you feel so weak your legs collapse. Samson was not personally equipped to rip the lion's jaws apart. But the Holy Spirit was—and is. You are not personally equipped to rip apart the jaws of whatever has power over you. You need strength other than your own. You need the strength of the Holy Spirit.

Marilyn Meberg,
Assurance for a Lifetime

"GOD WILLING"

The world is passing away . . .
but he who does the will of God abides forever.

1 JOHN 2:17

When I was a child, I learned a few common abbreviations that floated around in Christian circles. PTL meant "praise the Lord" and TLC meant "tender loving care." In school, girls would sign their notes BFF for "Best Friends Forever." In these days of email and chat rooms, abbreviations are more and more commonplace. LOL means "laugh out loud" and BRB means "be right back."

Long enough ago that many of us have forgotten, Christians used similar abbreviations in their hand-written letters—D.V. These two letters stand for the Latin words *Deo valente*, which basically mean "God willing." Holiday plans, promised visits, and travel arrangements would all be followed by the two little letters, D.V. It was a way of reminding each other that their lives were in God's hands, and their paths would follow God's will.

Christa Kinde, *Discovering God's Will for Your Life*

THE LORD'S RETURN

Be strong and take heart and wait for the LORD.

PSALM 27:14

Here in Southern California, one of the places where we have to do a lot of waiting is in traffic jams. The only good thing about going nowhere on one of our multilane freeways is that it gives me a good excuse to let my mind completely wander. (Of course, it sometimes wanders off completely, leaving me sitting there wondering where it's wandered to!)

Whenever I'm stuck in traffic or forced to do some waiting, I head off on a different path—mental path, that is. My favorite "mind trips" take me right up to heaven. I love to think about what it will be like when the trumpet toots and we scoot out of here. Even though millions of us will be flying away to meet Jesus in the clouds, isn't it nice to think there will be no traffic jams to contend with? That thought gives us the endurance we need to cling to the *first* part of Psalm 27:14 while enduring the second part: "Be strong and take heart and wait for the LORD."

Barbara Johnson, *Leaking Laffs*

WAIT ON THE LORD

*Commit your way to the LORD, trust also in Him,
and He shall bring it to pass.*

PSALM 37:5

I've often wondered why I've had to go through some difficulties repeatedly, and I believe it could be my inability to tarry with the Lord. I've gone through misunderstandings that have taken years to heal; I have gone through losses that I am still recovering from; and I have been forced to wait for others to change. What I'm learning is I'm not in control of this world, the choices of others, or even my own destiny. Now that is not easy to live with, especially for a right-now-gal.

I wonder if that's how Sarah felt when she decided to "help" God by giving Abraham her handmaiden Hagar to bear children. The end result of Sarah's refusal to wait on the Lord's timing is still being felt in the Jewish and Arab world today. If Sarah had known how her meddling in God's business would work out, I have a feeling she would gladly have found a quiet spot and waited.

Patsy Clairmont, *Women of Faith Devotional Bible*

A COVERING OF MERCY

*Our heart shall rejoice in Him,
because we have trusted in His holy name.*

PSALM 33:21

Have you ever been so disappointed in life that you have seemingly lost hope? More than that, have you ever found yourself hating hope? I can remember my mom lying in the hospital, her body ravaged by cancer. Many times I had hoped for healing that did not come. Did I dare hope again? Our humanness cries out to the God of the universe, "Why, why, why? Why should I hope? It doesn't work." Or does it?

Through many tears I have learned hope is based on eternal issues, not temporal ones. David shows us it is not just our minds or even our hearts that wait for the Lord. It is our very souls. And by hoping we receive the wonderful covering of God's mercy and grace—the only covering that can bring peace and inner joy.

Kathy Troccoli, *Women of Faith Devotional Bible*

JUMP FOR JOY!

Be glad in the LORD and rejoice, you righteous; and shout for joy, all you upright in heart!

PSALM 32:11

Don't you love being around children who are wiggling, squirming, jumping up and down, and shouting for joy? I do! I believe God does, too.

In fact, I believe God wants us to exhibit that same childlike joy as we worship and enjoy Him. I'm not talking about "feel-good" emotionalism that fluctuates with circumstances. I'm talking about deep down joy that bubbles up out of a grateful heart that knows and loves Jesus. That is the kind of heart that is instructed to rejoice in the Lord.

Happiness depends on *something*. Joy depends on *Someone*.

Sara Trollinger, *Women of Faith Devotional Bible*

ECSTATIC PEACE

Let the peace of God rule in your hearts, to which also you were called in one body; and be thankful.

COLOSSIANS 3:15

Years ago I had adopted a routine that robbed me of every ounce of peace I had received through faith in Christ. I rose early for work and stayed late to do more work. I had swallowed the lie that to "make it" in today's fast paced world, I had no other options. Peace evaporated. Ambition became an exacting master. After a company upheaval the hateful pant of career-collapse breathed down my neck. All of my sacrifices for an unfeeling corporation had been in vain.

I remember the night Christ led me gently back to His Word. As I drank in the Scriptures, they flowed into my desert of a heart like a slow, pleasing trickle of delight. I spoke candidly to God. In that single defining moment I had an astonishing revelation. Simple trust had been the missing factor in my spiritual equation. To know peace, all I had to do was trust God for the outcome. Complete trust equals complete peace—ecstatic peace.

Patricia Hickman, *Women of Faith Devotional Bible*

UNIQUELY YOU

*May He grant you according to your heart's desire,
and fulfill all your purpose.*

PSALM 20:4

I asked my son if he would like to paint his
room. Then I followed up with this ridiculous
question: "What color do you want to paint it?"
(Never ask a five-year-old-boy what color he
wants to paint his room!) He wanted it blue with
yellow polka dots and green stripes.

"All of it?" I asked, hoping that he would say,
"No, just the closet."

"All of it," he replied with hearty conviction.
"Every wall." And so we began.

The more I think about that experience the
more I celebrate the fact that this is how God is
with each of us. The great Master Painter allows
you and me to take up our little brushes and
paint our lives in a multitude of colors—some
that clash, some that takes others by
surprise or provoke disapproval. In all of
this He looks down on us in love,
He smiles, He celebrates our uniqueness.

Sheila Walsh, *The Great Adventure*

Truth On Duty

O Lord; let Your lovingkindness and Your truth continually preserve me.

PSALM 40:11

My son once quipped that packaged cupcakes have a longer shelf life than the Sequoia Redwoods. He added, "I don't want to eat anything that is going to last longer than I am." And while we don't like food petrified with additives, we do find preservation desirable, especially our own. David announces in Psalm 40 that truth acts as a preserving agent.

Preserve means "to hide, to watch (like a watchman would his vineyard), to inspect, to keep, to maintain." Therefore, truth troubleshoots in our behalf. *Continually* means "daily, morning and evening, without interruption. Truth is on duty "twenty-four seven."

"Tender Lord Jesus, we know we can't keep ourselves, and we ask that Your lovingkindness and truth be the additives that preserve us. Your constancy is our security. Amen."

Patsy Clairmont, *Women of Faith Devotional Bible*

THE EVERLASTING ARMS

The eternal God is your refuge,
and underneath are the everlasting arms.

DEUTERONOMY 33:27

When we're struggling through problems here on earth, trying to cope with the trials that block our way home, God longingly waits for us to turn to Him. God is there with us wherever we are on the road of life. He is our comfort today as well as our hope for tomorrow." "This is a strange journey we walk," one friend wrote to me, "Full of peaks and valleys. But since God is in both places, *we walk unafraid.*"

What could be more encouraging than remembering that we're loved by the almighty One who created us—and died for us! What could be more rewarding than the knowledge that the Carpenter from Nazareth has built mansions for us in heaven! And those inspiring facts are just part of the reason why heaven will be so wonderful.

Barbara Johnson, *Leaking Laffs*

FIRM IN HIS STRENGTH

Cast your burden on the LORD, and He shall sustain you; He shall never permit the righteous to be moved.

PSALM 55:22

Because loyalty and friendship were cherished by David, he became overwhelmed with grief when one of his close friends and companions betrayed him.

How do we respond when someone we love and trust abandons us? What did David do? He called upon God evening, morning, and noon. He prayed and cried aloud. In this way he cast his burden upon the Lord and learned this precious truth: When the hurt and pain are given to God, then the Lord is able to sustain and support us. Without the burden, we can stand firm in the strength of His might and not be moved—not be destroyed emotionally or spiritually or be moved from our trust in God or others.

Cynthia Heald, *Women of Faith Devotional Bible*

HEALTHY HUMILITY

God resists the proud, but gives grace to the humble.

JAMES 4:6

One of the keys to living the Christian life is to have healthy humility and to be ever aware of the dangers of subtle pride. The minute we begin to believe our own publicity, we are in for a nasty slide. The moment we feel we are invincible, the enemy crawls through one of the cracks of our pride and delights in showing us otherwise. Pride can be so subtle. It always begins with lies—the little comforting lies that we tell ourselves: "You're not like everybody else. You're strong. It'll never happen to you."

The truth is that we are all flawed creatures, and if we crawl out from under the protective wing of the Lord, we are most vulnerable. As Joy Dawson, author and speaker, said, "There are no extraordinary Christians—only ordinary Christians who serve an extraordinary God."

Sheila Walsh, *Life Is Tough but God Is Faithful*

OUR WILL OR GOD'S WILL?

You He made alive, who were dead in trespasses and sins.

EPHESIANS 2:1

With honed skill and honeyed words, the world tells us that we should follow our fancy. If it looks good, tastes good, sounds good, or feels good, then we need it. Never mind if it is *actually* good for us! According to these master salesmen, we need to awaken our senses (Nescafe®). That way we'll know that life tastes good (Coca-Cola®). Of course we deserve a break today (McDonalds®). Then, we should obey our thirst (Sprite®). Why? Because I'm worth it (L'Oreal®). After all, you know you want to (Pringles®). So just do it (Nike®)!

But the Bible reminds us that we used to live to fulfill the desires of our hearts and minds (Eph. 2:3), but no more! Now we need to place our will in subjection to God's will. Unfortunately, the world around us provides a big cheering section for self and selfish desires. Our choices are very important, because in the battle between our will and God's will, we get to decide who wins!

Christa Kinde, *Discovering God's Will for Your Life*

PLANT SOMETHING BETTER

Whatever is born of God overcomes the world.
And this is the victory that
has overcome the world—our faith.

1 JOHN 5:4

When I pull weeds from my flowerbeds, I've learned to plant something better in the vacancies left in the ground. If I don't, something just as bad or worse grows back in that place.

I have known people who have turned from a life of deep sin to become Christians. Many have left the bondage to some kind of addiction. But the people who grow the most are the ones who quickly plant something better in the vacancies of their lives through prayer, Bible reading, and Christian fellowship.

If you know someone who is a new Christian, show that person how to plant something better in the spot left by their former bondage. Teach them how to find God's lovingkindness. Share some of the fruits you have grown in your own life through the liberty you have found. Then rejoice together at the new beauty that will grow.

Lynda Hunter-Bjorklund, *Women of Faith Devotional Bible*

FAITH FOR A LIFETIME   191

Our Source of Contentment

Therefore let us pursue the things which make for peace and the things by which one may edify another.

ROMANS 14:19

There are some things that are really hard to do at the same time as something else. The classic example would be patting you head and rubbing you tummy. Let's see what else fits into that category? Laughing and keeping a straight face. Wearing white and eating spaghetti. Pouting and raising your eyebrows. Eating saltine crackers and whistling. And the ultimate impossible combination—focusing on Jesus and keeping track of everyone else.

When we are searching for contentment in our lives, we are easily derailed by our tendency to compare our lives to those around us. To take a step in cultivating the contentment quotient in your heart, pray for the ability to focus your attention on Jesus instead. He is your source of contentment, and He is your pattern for living contentedly.

Christa Kinde, *Cultivating Contentment*

GRACE AND GLORY

The LORD God is a sun and shield; the LORD will give grace and glory; no good thing will He withhold from those who walk uprightly.

PSALM 84:11

I'm embarrassed at how often I've heard myself say, "Oh, God, please. . . ." I learned to beg with my mother, so I employ those same techniques with God. To my relief, it never works.

You see, God's Word says He is a sun and a shield. A sun provides light so we can see. And a shield protects us from what we can't see. He has the grace to give us both.

I've learned God is *full* of grace. He withholds nothing that is good for me. I walk with Him; He shows me the way. I have a need; He provides it. When it isn't the fulfillment of my own imaginings, I trust Him. He sees the end from the beginning. He has the grace to give me what I need, and the grace to not. He's *full* of grace.

Mary Graham, *Women of Faith Devotional Bible*

OUR TRUE CALLING

Oh, send out Your light and Your truth!
Let them lead me.

PSALM 43:3

It takes courage to map out our own trail and find ways of living our lives and serving God that are a perfect fit for us.

I went to seminary to train to be a missionary to India, but it didn't take long to realize that was not what I wanted to do. It was actually what I thought I would hate, but I erroneously assumed that "sacrificing" myself by doing what I perceived as the ultimate Christian ministry would win the approval of God and others. I risked letting go of that self-imposed ideal and soon found myself on a new path as the first female evangelist with Youth for Christ. And that was just the beginning of all God had in mind for me.

It can feel risky to set aside old ideas and expectations, but when we move forward with the aid of divine guidance, we will discover our true calling.

Sheila Walsh, *The Great Adventure*

JOYFUL SOUNDS

Blessed are the people who know the joyful sound!
They walk . . . in the light of Your countenance.
In Your name they rejoice all day long.

PSALM 89:15–16

Every now and then, when things aren't going right, I check out what I'm listening to. What does the background of my life sound like? Television sitcoms? News reports? Gossip? Grumbling? If I can answer yes to any of those, then usually I presume a correlation, and I do my best to change the station to one that shouts out joy.

We tend to think our day is shaped by what we think, see, and do. But the sound of our lives is equally important. On those days when the background noise of my life isn't what it should be, I slip in a worship CD, listen for the giggle of my young son, or concentrate on the still small voice of God encouraging me, leading me on. All of these are joyful sounds, and with them I'll walk in the light of God's countenance.

Karen Kingsbury,
Women of Faith Devotional Bible

No Grit and Grime

*Enter into His gates with thanksgiving,
and into His courts with praise.*

PSALM 100:2

I used to live a ninety minute drive from the beach. Often the family would head out for a day of fun in the sun and sand and enjoy a picnic and swim. But I also remember the long drive home that same evening. With the stings of sunburn, eyes burning from the salt water, arms and legs sticky and gritty from tunnels and sandcastles, the family got grouchier as the miles wore on. Nothing felt better than stepping into a hot shower and washing all the grit and salt away. Clean and fresh once again, moods lifted.

We need much the same transformation when we come before God's presence. We need to shower off the grit and grime that distract our attention and shift our focus to the things that generate a real celebration: gratefulness that He lets us serve His purposes here on earth. Gratefulness that He is always there waiting—no matter what mood we're experiencing.

Dianna Booher, *Women of Faith Devotional Bible*

WE WANT FORGIVENESS

You have forgiven the iniquity of Your people;
You have covered all their sin.

PSALM 85:2

One of my favorite definitions of forgiveness
is "giving up your right to punish." That
always seemed to make good sense to me because
my natural bent when hurt is to punish the one
who has done the hurting. Can you relate? Sort of
that "eye for an eye and tooth for a tooth" thing.
That makes perfect sense to me until I'm the one
in need of forgiveness. Then I really don't want to
be reminded of what I've done, and I really don't
want to be punished. I want the one who has
anything against me to send it away from me and
give up her right to punish me.

You see, we all want forgiveness. It is a blessed
state. That is why it is so gratifying to know that
God has forgiven us. He has sent our offenses far
away from us by putting them on His Son, Jesus
Christ. He also has given up His right to punish us.
We are forgiven. That is what makes us members of
His kingdom—His kingdom of forgiveness.

Jan Silvious, *Women of Faith Devotional Bible*

REMOVING THE BARRIERS

As far as the east is from the west, so far has He removed our transgressions from us.

PSALM 103:12

Two big barriers exist in many Christians' lives: unforgiveness and guilt.

Unforgiveness keeps us from being able to share what's good in our lives, and guilt causes us continual pain. I've met so many moms and dads who are unable to forgive their adult children for the pain they've caused their parents—and those same parents are often wracked with guilt thinking they are somehow to blame for their children's problems. Sometimes these feelings are so entrenched there is no way humanly possible to get out of the pit they've created.

Only God can bring about changes in our hearts. As Psalm 103:8–14 reminds us, when we have wronged and disappointed Him, we ask forgiveness and He grants it. He removes our mistakes and guilt "as far as the east is from the west." Then He waits for us to do the same to those who have wronged and disappointed us.

Barbara Johnson, *Women of Faith Devotional Bible*

GOD MAKES NO JUNK!

I am fearfully and wonderfully made; marvelous are Your works, and that my soul knows very well.

PSALM 139:14

Even before Adam was created, God already had us on His mind and had determined our birthdays, our mommas and daddies, our looks, our responses to life, and even when we would die. God was thinking about us when there was only form and void in the world. And He has never stopped thinking about us.

The psalmist describes that God made every intricate part of our beings, like a master weaver who takes the finest silk threads and makes a priceless garment with precision, excellence, and exquisitely great taste. The recipient of the garment has the ability to accept this unique treasure with dignity.

Yes, that's who you are. You are a creation of God, made with His character, crafted with His DNA, and loved unconditionally by Him. God never makes junk!

Thelma Wells,
Women of Faith Devotional Bible

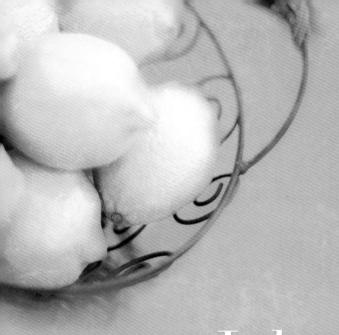

July

The only source of true love
is God.

The Perfect Christian Walk

We also glory in tribulations,
knowing that tribulation produces perseverance; and
perseverance, character; and character, hope.

ROMANS 5:3–4

When I picture myself in the perfect Christian walk, I see a woman who is patient and wise. She is completely faithful in studying the Word. She is committed to prayer. She always knows just what to do, what to say, and how to react. She is loving, compassionate, and confident in sharing her faith with others. My ideal life doesn't involve any bumps or scrapes. I'd really find it easier to be content if life would move along smoothly and without surprises. Wouldn't you think God would be pleased by those noble desires?

Actually, I don't think God is impressed with my daydreams. Wishing for perfection doesn't accomplish the Lord's work in me. He can use me, just as I am, so long as I am willing to be used. And all those trials I have to go through serve His purposes in making me grow into the person He wants me to become.

Christa Kinde, *Cultivating Contentment*

Words Set the Tone

*Cause me to hear Your lovingkindness in the morning,
for in You do I trust.*

PSALM 143:8

Words impact our lives at deeper levels than we at times acknowledge. Words can set the tone for a day. They can build faith and hope or despair and uncertainty. They can wound, and they can heal.

Each morning we get to choose what will be the first thing we take into our hearts. We can switch on the television and hear of wars and rumors of wars, of human suffering and moral decay, or we can bathe ourselves—heart and soul—in the Word of God. We can't isolate ourselves from what is going on around us every day, but we decide who has the first word.

Sheila Walsh, *Women of Faith Devotional Bible*

PRAYING THE PSALMS

My voice You shall hear in the morning, O LORD; in the morning I will direct it to You, and I will look up.

PSALM 5:3

The book of Psalms is a compilation of prayers that were meant to be prayed aloud. They are a tremendous comfort to those of you who feel you're not ready yet to open your mouth in prayer. You may feel your words won't sound good enough. You'll see that there is nothing polished or refined about the language in the Psalms prayers. They are sometimes whiny, happy, confused, faltering, repetitious, and uncertain. In other words, the Psalms use real words to express real emotion. You can literally pray the Psalms to God. Choose one, then read it aloud to God as your expression to Him. In time, doing so will not feel awkward. You will find your own spirit uniting with the spirit of the words as if you had written them yourself.

Marilyn Meberg,
Assurance for a Lifetime

HEALTHY BODIES

Fear the LORD and depart from evil.
It will be health to your flesh, and strength to your bones.

PROVERBS 3:8

"Most people suffer poor health," the old saying goes, "not because of what they eat, but from what is eating them!"

Years before science linked healthy bodies and minds, Solomon wrote that humility, reverence, and righteous living would result in physical health. The grocery store newsstands abound with magazines to promote a healthy lifestyle, but how many of those consider a person's spiritual well-being?

Feeling stressed? Cast your cares upon the One who cares for you (see 1 Pet. 5:7). Exhausted? Run to the One whose yoke is easy and whose burden is light (see Matt. 11:30). Worried? Place your concerns in Jesus' hands and trust Him to meet your needs (see Matt. 6:25–26).

Angela Elwell Hunt, *Women of Faith Devotional Bible*

MORE LIKE CHRIST

*Our light affliction, which is but for a moment,
is working for us a far more
exceeding and eternal weight of glory.*

2 CORINTHIANS 4:17

God has not forgotten you. When God says no to a longing, it is because not filling it will shape us more than filling it would. These longings are in our lives to shape us by the wanting. We are becoming more like Christ, often by suffering, by being finely ground.

The happiest women I know are the spiritually mature. They aren't giddy happy, they are free happy. Their marriages are good, but they are not everything they ever longed for. They look to God to meet their ultimate needs. They are not free from disappointment, but they bring their disappointment to Christ, trusting that He is using it in their lives. That's the kind of trust I want, and the kind of woman I want to be.

Nicole Johnson, *Fresh-Brewed Life*

A GARMENT OF LOVE

Hatred stirs up strife, but love covers all sins.

PROVERBS 10:12

It is easy to love the friend who is our encourager, standing on the sideline of life, cheering us on. We elevate people's value to us based upon how they make us feel about ourselves. To the booing section, those criticizing types who seem to delight in our mistakes, we withdraw our fondness. When we practice the act of love, covering up the ugly things said against us as though the offending tongue had simply made an innocent slip, we find the gentle garment of love draped over our own mistakes. Christ does this for us continually, covering us with the beauty of His own righteousness. Love is the act of sharing our undeserved covering, even with those who are not so lovable. Not only is unrequited love our responsibility, it is also our privilege as children of the King.

Patricia Hickman,
Women of Faith Devotional Bible

MISPLACED HOPE

*You are my hope, O Lord GOD; You are
my trust from my youth.*

PSALM 71:5

This week I experienced a major disappointment.
As I wrestled with the implications of this in
my heart, I fought hard to hold back tears when I
thought about losing what I had really been hoping
for. It's even fair to say I felt a little bit hopeless.

I'm humbled to write it, but I had misplaced
my hope. I was looking for it, and I couldn't find it
anywhere, because I had put it in the wrong place.
I had put more hope in the outcome of my situation
than in the God of the outcome of my situation.
I was afraid to trust God unless I could be sure
everything was going to turn out the way I thought
it should. That's where I had misplaced my hope.

I had to retrace my steps to discover where I
had carelessly set it down. I had put it down in the
center of my circumstances, and it just didn't belong
there. But I found it, and asked God to help me put
it back where I knew it belonged, with Him.

Nicole Johnson, *WOF Association Letters*

STRENGTH OUT OF WEAKNESS

Out of weakness [they] were made strong.

HEBREWS 11:34

Many ancient believers are members of the Bible's "Hall of Faith." But consider the character traits of these nominees for the Bible's "Hall of Weakness." Eve was a blame-shifter. Cain let anger and bitterness turn to hatred and murder. Noah had a weakness for wine. Abraham told lies to protect himself. Sarah was jealous of a younger woman. Rebekah played favorites with her children. Jacob was sly. Rachel was envious of her sister's successes. Moses was afraid to speak in public. Aaron succumbed to peer pressure. Samson was a womanizer. David tried to hide the evidence of his sins. Peter tended to speak before thinking. Thomas placed facts before faith.

Yet if you look at the end of the "Hall of Faith" in Hebrews 11, you will find a little phrase in the midst the volleys of praise. The writer states that these faithful men and women "out of weakness were made strong." So you see, they weren't so very different from us after all!

Christa Kinde, *Living In Jesus*

A Cash-Only Basis

There is one who makes himself rich, yet has nothing.

"Easy" credit is very seductive, and too many of us fall into its snare. Having worked in a bank, I know of people who got bill consolidation loans and kept their credit cards to boot. When they paid off their bills with the loan, they'd often stay straight for several months. But almost invariably, they'd go into a store one day, see something they thought they couldn't live without, and purchase it with one of those credit cards that should have been canceled when they got the loan. Girl, it doesn't take but a few times to impulse buy with a credit card before you're right back where you started or worse.

The fact is, you can't borrow your way out of debt. You've got to pay your way. So cut up all but one of your credit cards (for life-threatening emergencies only) and hide it in a plastic bag in your freezer under several pounds of ice! From now on, pay cash for anything you buy. If you don't have the cash, don't get the product.

Thelma Wells, *Girl, Have I Got Good News for You*

LIVING BY FAITH

The life which I now live in the flesh I live by faith in the Son of God, who loved me and gave Himself for me.

GALATIANS 2:20

Real ongoing, lifelong education doesn't answer questions—it provokes them. It causes us to see that the fun and excitement of learning doesn't lie in having all the answers. It lies in the tension and the stretching of our minds between all the contradictory answers. It makes us think for ourselves. It frees us. It helps us grow up!

Even Scripture doesn't tell us every single thing we'd like to know. While it serves as a standard for living and a chart for life's course, much of it remains a secret. God designed it that way and that's okay. In fact, recently I heard my brother Chuck say during one of his Insight for Living broadcasts, "I find myself very comfortable when I come to Scripture that doesn't answer everything." I do too. That keeps us dependent upon God and having to live by faith. Fun, isn't it? And the fun's never going to stop!

Luci Swindoll, *You Bring the Confetti*

WELL-INTENDED WORDS

A word fitly spoken is like
apples of gold in settings of silver.

PROVERBS 25:11

"If the shoe fits . . . buy two pair," someone quipped. Now that's good advice. It isn't easy to find a comfortable fit. It's true of words as well. Some words pinch, cause discomfort, and blister our self-esteem. But a good fit—a gracious word—comforts our minds and emotions like an old pair of house slippers on work-weary feet.

Some of the most hurtful situations in my life have been spiteful words I have both ranted and regretted, or either had slung in my direction, leaving me crushed. And yet some of my most touching and meaningful moments have been well-placed, well-suited, well-intended words that I either spoke or received.

Grace-filled word investors are worth their weight in silver and gold. If the (gracious) word fits . . . say it!

Patsy Clairmont, *Women of Faith Devotional Bible*

ONE STANDARD

The integrity of the upright will guide them,
but the perversity of the unfaithful will destroy them.

PROVERBS 11:3

There's an old joke that goes something like this: Every business owner has three sets of books: 1. the set of figures given to the IRS; 2. the actual figures; and 3. the actual hours and revenue billed to clients. Although the punch line generates a laugh, the scenario is repeated in a thousand ways in our society.

In general, standards, truths, and absolutes seem to have gone the way of eight-track tapes and leisure suits. But God's Word is the standard we must all measure our lives by. One standard. One truth. No protests. No exceptions.

Dianna Booher, *Women of Faith Devotional Bible*

JULY 13

God's Plan and Purpose

*A man's heart plans his way,
but the LORD directs his steps.*

PROVERBS 16:9

There are two things I might've changed about my life: I wouldn't have been the youngest in a family of eight (although I can't decide which sibling I could live without!), and I wouldn't have grown up poor.

But we don't always know what we might need in life. There are many positive aspects of my adult life that I can directly attribute to growing up in my family of origin, in our tiny little town.

Because I was little, I learned to speak up. Because I was young, I learned to keep up. And because I was last, I learned to make up the difference. All of that has served me well through the years. When I'm in over my head, I'm comfortable reaching. When I'm overwhelmed, I keep going. When I'm overcommitted, I hang on. Just like my siblings did. God has His purpose for everything.

Mary Graham, *Women of Faith Devotional Bible*

LOOKING FOR LOVE

A new commandment I give to you,
that you love one another; as I have loved you.

JOHN 13:34

The six o'clock news is filled with tales of abusive love, perverted love, and unrequited love. And our entertainment— whoa!—temporary love, lust disguised as love, destructive love, thin-as-tissue-paper love that lasts six months, then calls it quits. Those stories aren't really about love at all.

Our world is fixated on love because we're so desperate to experience it. Trouble is, we keep missing the mark because we're looking for love in all the wrong places. We're looking for love within each other, when the only source of true love is God. The only way we can experience real love with each other is through Him.

Angela Elwell Hunt,
Women of Faith Devotional Bible

THE SAVIOR IS WAITING

*You shall know that I, the LORD, am your Savior
and your Redeemer, the Mighty One of Jacob.*

ISAIAH 60:16

We live in a culture that is extremely "me" focused. Me first. My stuff. My life. My way. But life has a way of bringing us to our knees. When life deals a hurting blow, we realize that we don't know all the answers. But that's a good thing. A weak man is never so strong as when he reaches up to God for help and healing. The end of yourself is where healing begins. The Savior waits for you. Isn't it interesting? In times of distress we find that it's not at all about us. It's all about Jesus.

Babbie Mason, *Women of Faith Devotional Bible*

STRONG AND STEADY

*"My grace is sufficient for you,
for My strength is made perfect in weakness."*

2 CORINTHIANS 12:9

Strength is such a manly quality. It's hard for a lady to wrap her arms around a description like "tough as nail" or "strong as an ox." No woman wants to be compared to an ox! Though most of us are not "mighty oaks," we do possess God-given strengths. We would just word them a little differently.

How about "strong as Aunt Edna's coffee" or "steady as a pair of orthopedic shoes." Maybe you are as strong as super-hold hairspray or as durable as name-brand paper towels. Many women face sacrifice and service daily. Nobody notices their steadiness. No one admires them for their dedication. There is a quiet strength in women that enables them to do the thing that is in front of them. The strength you have may be small, but serve the Lord with all you have. Give Him all you've got!

Christa Kinde, *Living In Jesus*

THE FAMILY OF GOD

*"My mother and My brothers are
these who hear the word of God and do it."*

LUKE 8:21

Family is so important. Within the family you have those who have big dreams and those who like to daydream. There are those who need more attention than those who are ultra independent. There are those who trust God for everything and those who attempt to be more logical. There are those who are hilarious and those who are serious. There are those who love to cook and those who just love to eat. But whatever the differences are, there is one force that keeps family close and together, the bloodline. It's been said that blood is thicker than water.

In the family of God, there is a bond deep inside that binds us one to the other. It is the glue of authentic love expressing itself in caring for, clinging to, and coming to the aid of each other without strings attached. It is the river of love streaming from the bloodline of our Savior that finds, fetches, and fastens us one to the other.

Thelma Wells, *WOF Association Letters*

PROGRESS AND GROWTH

*Grow in the grace and knowledge
of our Lord and Savior Jesus Christ.*

2 PETER 3:18

Here's the age old question, "Where do the years go?" Scripture puts our timeline this way: "It is but a breath and then it's gone."

My parents used to tell me I'd have to wait until later for things I wanted—back then "later" seemed to stretch into centuries. Today I am amazed at how quickly the year goes between mammograms. Groan. Not that again.

Yes, things change with the passage of time—and so do people. Or do we? Change is not easy. Old habits are hard to break; new patterns are challenging to incorporate and maintain. Yet I don't want to settle into my retirement rocking chair and realize one day that I am the same ornery gal I was in my twenties. (Okay, okay, since birth.) I want to be able to chart measurable progress and growth. I want to be kinder, sweeter, and wiser. Hmm. I'd better hurry.

Patsy Clairmont, *WOF Association Letters*

FORGIVE AND BLESS

If you do not forgive men their trespasses,
neither will your Father forgive your trespasses.

MATTHEW 6:15

Is there anything more painful than being hurt by a friend? When a friend in the ministry offended me, I had a difficult time wanting to forgive her. Yet I knew if I held unforgiveness in my heart, the Lord wouldn't hear my prayers. I began to pray and ask God to forgive her because I didn't feel like forgiving her myself. Even then, it was hard to dismiss the negative thoughts that popped into my mind. But whenever those thoughts surfaced, God reminded me to pray for her to be blessed, as I wanted to be blessed. I did. Within a few weeks, the healing came.

Is there someone in your life who has hurt you? Ask God to forgive and bless that person—even if you don't feel like it. In time, your own healing and willingness to forgive will come.

Sara Trollinger,
Women of Faith Devotional Bible

OVERCOMING FEAR

"Fear not, for I am with you; be not dismayed,
for I am your God. . . . I will uphold you
with My righteous right hand."

ISAIAH 41:10

One evening in October of 2001, I found myself lying under my rickety, metal-frame bed inside a pitch-black Afghan prison cell, with bombs exploding nearby. They created such a force, even our prison walls were shaking. My stomach tied in knots, unable to sleep, and uncertain if I would live through the night, I found myself gripped with fear. Fear immobilized me; it paralyzed me. Fear robbed me of peace, and I felt overwhelmed. In that moment, I did the only thing I knew to do to overcome the fear. I called on the name of Jesus! "Jesus," I prayed, "please come and lie down next to me and give me peace." The moment I called on His name, His presence came and tangibly comforted me under the bed in that cold cell. Though my circumstances did not change, I found peace in the One who alone is unchanging!

Heather Mercer, *Women of Faith Devotional Bible*

GOD CARES FOR OUR CHILDREN

*"All your children shall be taught by the LORD, and
great shall be the peace of your children."*

ISAIAH 54:13

If you asked me what my biggest recurrent
worry in life has been, I would likely say, "My
children." Those two, small, eight-pound wonders
have never been far from my thoughts since the
day they were born—and they are now nearly
grown! Most mothers would agree. Nothing quite
rattles our cages like a child who is struggling or
one who has strayed from his faith. Nothing so
disturbs our peace of mind.

Perhaps that is why Isaiah 54:13 has been
claimed by mothers through the ages, over and
over. God speaks right to the core of our concern.
What a peace is ours when we realize God
Himself has promised to carry the responsibility
for our children! They were His before they
became ours. He will be their teacher. He will
establish them in righteousness and peace.

Paula Rinehart, *Women of Faith Devotional Bible*

OUT OF THE BOX

*"With men this is impossible,
but with God all things are possible."*

MATTHEW 19:26

Jesus is unconventional. He'll work in ways you may not recognize or understand. And He is big enough to do the things you have labeled impossible.

He has enough power.

He has enough time.

He is bigger than your problem.

Believe in Him more than in what you may see. Trust in Him more than what you may feel. You can question. He can handle your questions. God is highly confident of His own plans. He can do everything but fail.

Kathy Troccoli, *Hope for a Woman's Heart*

We Celebrate God

*Let us continually offer the sacrifice
of praise to God, that is, the fruit of our lips,
giving thanks to His name.*

HEBREWS 13:15

The wisdom and doctrine of Scripture teach
that the experience of celebrating God is the
core of worship. It is the quintessence of praise
and thanksgiving—the most perfect manifestation
of a heart that gratefully fellowships with the One
who provides life and all the gifts of living. In
fact, a grateful heart is not only the greatest
virtue, it is the seed bed for all other virtues.
When we are caught up in the celebration of God
there is neither room nor time for the invasion of
negative living. As we rejoice before the Lord, as
we serve Him in the area of our calling, as we
enter joyfully into our daily journey, as we give
thanks to Him for His kindness and
faithfulness, we celebrate God.

Luci Swindoll, *You Bring the Confetti*

CHILDLIKE FAITH

Faith is the substance of things hoped for,
the evidence of things not seen.

HEBREWS 11:1

The rope swing in our back yard was tied securely to a high branch in a towering old box elder tree. It was a long length of nylon rope, with a simple loop tied at the bottom. One foot could be placed in the loop, or you could simply sit on the knot. To make this amusement more exciting, my Dad propped an old ladder against one of the lower branches of the tree. My sister and I would take turns grabbing the loop of the rope swing, scampering up as high as we'd dare on the ladder, putting our foot in the loop, grabbing tight, and launching ourselves into the air.

As a child, I trusted in my Dad's rope-tying abilities, I trusted the rope would hold me, I trusted the old tree branch to carry my weight. In fact, I trusted those things so much, that I never gave them a thought. No second-guessing or wondering why. Just grab on and jump! That's childlike faith.

Christa Kinde, *Living In Jesus*

God Comes Near

"I dwell in the high and holy place,
with him who has a contrite and humble spirit, . . .
to revive the heart of the contrite ones."

ISAIAH 57:15

What a picture of the beauty of God in that verse! The One who is high and lifted up in glory, whose robe fills the temple (see Isa. 6:1), is the same God who draws near to the humble and contrite of spirit. Though He is high and holy, He comes alongside broken people who turn to Him.

When life has rolled over you like a dump truck, how do you see God? Is He far removed, waiting for you to get up and dust yourself off? Isaiah declares that God comes near in the moments we would least expect. He breathes new life into our broken places. He takes us by the hand and comforts us. The One who inhabits eternity restores our souls.

Paula Rinehart,
Women of Faith Devotional Bible

JUST LOVE THEM

If God so loved us, we also ought to love one another.

1 JOHN 4:11

Show your children you love them by your actions. Don't nag your kids about their choices. If you do, they'll get to the place where they won't want to be around you. They already know how you feel about things. Don't wash their faces with your distaste. Just *love them.*

Baby, you cannot control your grown children. They are no longer babies; at their ages they will continue to make their own decisions, right or wrong. Keep your focus on who your son is becoming inside, not on what he looks like on the outside. Treat your daughter and her companion with godly love and respect. Pray for them that God will intervene and change both of their minds.

One of the deceased pastors of my church, Dr. Ernest C. Estell Sr., would say, "When your children are little, you talk to them about God. When they are grown, you talk to God about them."

Thelma Wells, *Girl, Have I Got Good News for You*

FEASTING ON GOD'S WORD

Your words were found, and I ate them, and Your
word was to me the joy and rejoicing of my heart.

JEREMIAH 15:16

When my children were young, they would head straight for the kitchen after walking in the door from school. The work and stress of the day seemed to melt away with once glance at a plate of cookies waiting on the counter.

Jeremiah wrote about similar appetites. He also headed to the "kitchen" to eat—or consume or devour—God's Word. We, too, will know we are walking closely with God when we find childlike joy in feasting daily, not only on Scripture, but also on the knowledge that Someone knows and loves us so much, He leaves a plate of goodies.

Lynda Hunter-Bjorklund,
Women of Faith Devotional Bible

Planted Next to Water

"Blessed is the man who trusts in the LORD,
for he shall be like a tree planted by the waters . . .
and will not be anxious in the year of drought,
nor will cease from yielding fruit."

JEREMIAH 17:7–8

I went on vacation one year and forgot to leave instructions for a friend to water my favorite tree—a miniature lilac planted on the west side of the house. When we got back, the little tree sort of resembled the Sahara desert—during a blight.

Jeremiah reminds us that we are blessed (or happy) when we put our hope and trust in the Lord. For then we will be like trees that are planted next to the water—sending our roots deep into the riverbed of God's Word, drawing the thirst-quenching, life-sustaining truth from the flow of His Spirit. Then and only then can we bear fruit for others to be nourished.

Lori Copeland,
Women of Faith Devotional Bible

THE RIGHT ROAD

What does the LORD require of you but to do justly,
to love mercy, and to walk humbly with your God?

MICAH 6:8

Life can be hard—and grossly unfair. When
the bad things happen, we often ask, "Can I
trust God?" But perhaps the real question is, "Can
God trust me?" Can He trust us to hold on? Can
He trust us to want to become mature Christians,
or will we remain little children who believe in
Him only if He makes it worth our while? When
life seems to cave in for no reason at all, will we
remember that God is faithful?

If we're going to be able to handle life when
it doesn't seem to make sense, we have to get real.
We have to set our faces in the right direction and
keep walking as He walked. At times the road will
be long and dark, the mountains unscalable.
Because we're human we won't always make
perfect choices. Sometimes it will seem we take
two steps forward and one step back, but it
doesn't really matter. All that really matters is
being on the right road.

Sheila Walsh, *Life Is Tough but God Is Faithful*

A Trustworthy Friend

The tongue of the wise uses knowledge rightly,
but the mouth of fools pours forth foolishness.

PROVERBS 15:1

"Friend" and "trustworthy" should go hand in hand. If you want to be a Big-Girl friend, then you have to choose to protect your friend's privacy and dignity for always. Sometimes that means keeping your mouth shut about something you know about your friend, even if you think it is harmless. You might find yourself in a group where others seem to know all about the issue, but out of respect for your friend, you keep quiet. Your friend's business is not everyone else's business.

My friend Carolyn is that kind of friend. I have seen her faithfully handle private information not only for me but for others for over thirty years. She can be trusted. If we ever share anything that is okay for us to discuss and is confidential we often say, "Now this is 'grave' talk." What we mean is that we will take the conversation to our grave.

Jan Silvious, *Big Girls Don't Whine*

OUR HEALER

Come, and let us return to the LORD;
for He has torn, but He will heal us; He has stricken,
but He will bind us up.

HOSEA 6:1

Have you ever taken a child to the emergency room and watched the doctor dig gravel or glass out of a bad cut or set a broken leg? Then you understand the doctor sometimes has to cause pain, even tear tissue, in the healing process. But you let the doctor continue, despite the child's protests, because you understand the healing that will come afterward.

God deals with us in the same way. The process may sometimes be painful, but the result is healing. Who would ever want to stay in a sickened, weakened, dirty condition when we can be well?

Dianna Booher, *Women of Faith Devotional Bible*

August

Christ died to give us life,
life right now.

SPENDING GOD'S PROMISES

"My people shall never be put to shame."

JOEL 2:26

I was born with a pulmonary defect that weakened the muscles around my heart. As my condition worsened, my mother was told that I would die before I started school. But one day, as a new Christian reading her Bible, Mom realized this news was contrary to Scripture she'd read such as, "My people shall never be put to shame." Mom decided to "spend" God's promises, and she went out and bought my school clothes and enrolled me in kindergarten.

Mom's faith was tested often as I continued to miss many days of school that year. At some point, however, things turned around, and I grew stronger. By the end of first grade, I had won a physical fitness award. In the years to come, free from all heart problems, I became the biggest tomboy in my family.

"My people shall never be put to shame." That meant my mom, and that means you and me.

Lynda Hunter-Bjorklund,
Women of Faith Devotional Bible

I Love a Challenge

*Man looks at the outward appearance,
but the LORD looks at the heart.*

1 SAMUEL 16:7

I was in London waiting for a train when a young man with spiked hair, leather clothes, and army boots walked on the platform. He had a mean look on his face.

I was seated on a bench holding my luggage. When I saw him coming and people shrinking back, I thought, *He's just gonna have to do to me whatever he wants. I'm so tired, I don't even care.* He sat down beside me, still looking as if he could kill somebody. As tired as I was, I said hello and asked how he was doing. Suddenly, he gave a half smile and answered me, and we began a conversation.

People stared at us in dismay. I suppose they were thinking, *Look at that old, black grandma and that weird, no-good derelict. They deserve each other.* If I had run from him as others did, I would have missed a marvelous opportunity for a friendly conversation. Sweetie, you just cannot judge a book by its cover.

Thelma Wells, *Girl, Have I Got Good News for You*

CAPTURE EACH MOMENT

*Behold, I am the LORD, the God of all flesh.
Is there anything too hard for Me?*

JEREMIAH 32:27

Every person is a combination of many factors woven together from the joys and sorrows of life. We're also the product of our choices. We're the result of what was or was not done for us or to us by our parents, siblings, associates, and friends. The journey we're on is planned and watched over by a loving God who wants us to treasure the gift of being alive and who sets us free to participate in our own destiny.

When we realize our lives are to be given away, everything about our outlook changes and grows. We see and do things differently as a result. We think beyond our own borders. The world becomes accessible through the power of God's spirit and love. We capture each moment, embrace the journey, and go forward.

Luci Swindoll,
I Married Adventure

Soul-Satisfying Nourishment

Oh, how I love Your law! It is my meditation all the day.

PSALM 119:97

When we moved into our most recent home, there were all of three trees in the yard— not nearly enough by our estimation. So every year we have added trees and shrubs around the property . . . a paper birch, a flowering dogwood, three crepe myrtles, and a whole row of Bradford pear. With each addition, we watched and watered carefully. My five-year-old son offered to help with the watering duties. Clutching the hose in two hands, he would aim the nozzle high, sending a shower of rain across the baby tree's leaves. He needed to be taught it was the roots that needed the water more. A slow and steady trickle of water at the base of a tree does much more good that a scatter of droplets across its leaves.

Are you getting nourishment from the Lord in erratic bursts that splash across your Sundays, or have you discovered the soul-satisfying nourishment of a steady supply from the Scriptures every day?

Christa Kinde, *Living In Jesus*

HOPE IN EVERY VALLEY

I have set the LORD always before me;
because He is at my right hand I shall not be moved.

PSALM 16:8

Life in Christ is not free of pain, problems, and PMS. No doubt, right now, you are experiencing problems in your life. We are! Complete joy is not about our circumstances. Complete joy is about confidence in God's love and purposes for us. We have hope in every valley for we know that, in His time, the boundary lines will be pleasant and the inheritance delightful. Even in the midst of enormous pain, we discover we can trust God and His way is perfect.

Though we still know suffering, though our constantly changing circumstances can cause pain, underneath is an unchanging joy. As we set the Lord always before us, we will not be shaken. That brings a divine confidence, which brings a divine peace, which opens wide the window to let in a divine joy.

Dee Brestin and Kathy Troccoli, *The Colors of His Love*

OPEN THE SHUTTERS!

*The eyes of the LORD are on the righteous,
and His ears are open to their cry.*

PSALM 34:15

Have you ever thought how hopeful it is to see the sunrise? Not that I'm always up to see it, or if I'm up, not that I always have the presence of mind to "see" it. But I saw it this morning, and it was a real gift of hope. It reminds me that this is a new day, and that there are always new and fresh beginnings. It whispers to my heart that sorrow may last for the night, but joy arrives like a sunrise in the morning.

I feel like the essence of my calling may be wrapped up in the sunrise. So many women walk in very dark, hard circumstances. They feel hopeless. The shutters of their hearts are closed and boarded up. My greatest joy is to write drama that somehow rips the boards off and throws open the shutters and lets the light come in to pierce the darkness. Fortunately, I do not have to make the light, or be the light—that is what God does with His beauty and grace.

Nicole Johnson, *WOF Association Letters*

COME AS YOU ARE

He who comes to Me shall never hunger,
and he who believes in Me shall never thirst.

JOHN 6:35

My son, Christian, loves cupcakes. I frost them with a dark chocolate frosting. One day I was going out and had on a white cotton blouse and jeans. He saw me come into the kitchen and yelled, "Mom!" and threw his arms around my neck and rubbed his grubby little face in my hair.

I thought, *This is how God invites us to come to Him. Not to clean ourselves up, but to come and bury our face in the mane of the Lion of Judah. Come as we really are.* It wouldn't cross Christian's mind to clean up before he hugged me because I have on a white blouse.

Our heavenly Father doesn't require that we clean up before we come to Him. We can come just as we are—with all our imperfections and doubts. He just wants us to come.

Sheila Walsh, *Life Is Tough but God Is Faithful*

THE FINAL OUTCOME

The just shall live by his faith.

HABAKKUK 2:4

The first time I watched my daughter's state basketball tournament, I worried that her team would lose. Now I relax, eat popcorn, and enjoy the reruns of the state win with confidence because I know the final outcome.

I'm learning to see life's challenges through similar eyes. By looking back on what God has done, I trust Him more for what He will do. My mother says, "We know who wins because we've read the end of the Book."

To me, faith means relaxing, eating my popcorn, and enjoying the game with confidence, no matter how close the score gets.

Lynda Hunter-Bjorklund,
Women of Faith Devotional Bible

LIGHTS ON THE HILLSIDE

Let your light so shine before men, that they may
see your good works and glorify your Father in heaven.

MATTHEW 5:16

The basic purpose for living is to glorify our Father in heaven. We who believe in Him are lights on a hillside, seen from a distance. We are to cast vision, give warmth, and show a better way to those living in darkness. In short, God instructs us to shine. How do we do that?

Encourage instead of criticize. Love instead of hate. Hope instead of doubt. Give instead of take. Trust instead of worry.

We open our hearts to others so they will be prompted to open their hearts to God. Encouragement, love, hope, generosity, and trust are all gifts of God by the work of His Spirit. They don't spring from our humanity; they spring from His grace. God gives the light. He uses us to show the way. And He is glorified.

Luci Swindoll, *Women of Faith Devotional Bible*

HE PAID OUR DEBT

In Him we have redemption through His blood, the
forgiveness of sins, according to the riches of His grace.

EPHESIANS 1:7

I drove up to the parking attendant's small booth and handed her my parking stub. She raised her eyebrows, smiled with surprise, and asked for my autograph. Humbled that she would even recognize me, I obliged her request. She took no money from me, but thanked me and raised the gate, wishing me a blessed day. Although my debt was minimal, she cancelled it and sent me away rejoicing.

Sin kept us locked up in a prison of misery and bondage. But Christ recognized our plight, paid a debt He did not owe, forgave our sin, and sent us freely on our way rejoicing.

Babbie Mason, *Women of Faith Devotional Bible*

ONLY BELIEVE

He said to her, "Daughter, your faith has made you well. Go in peace, and be healed of your affliction."

MARK 5:34

We do not know this woman's social standing, only that she had spent all of her money in hope of being well again. Her desperation sent her reaching through the crowd to find that thing she needed—healing. She didn't ask the Lord with words, nor did she have the luxury of time on her side. In front of her was a miracle-working Source. Without hesitation she seized the opportunity, pressing through the mob where her fingers reached out for Christ's clothing. Thinking she would operate her faith in secrecy, like some cosmic hit-and-run maneuver, she was surprised when Jesus directed all attention onto her. Red-faced and uncomfortable with her sudden moment in the limelight, she explained her belief in His power to heal her, even through a Carpenter's robe. Pleased by her extraordinary example, Christ sent her home cured. She had found the secret to pleasing God: only believe.

Patricia Hickman, *Women of Faith Devotional Bible*

EXTEND FORGIVENESS

*Whenever you stand praying, if you have anything
against anyone, forgive him, that your
Father in heaven may also forgive you your trespasses.*

MARK 11:25

Through my children, I have learned that
forgiveness is not free—it costs the one who
forgives. When my children were young, the cost
of forgiving their mishaps was small—the
disappointment of a shattered vase, the effort
of scrubbing a crayon-scribbled wall. As my
children grew older, however, I paid for their
mishaps with the agony of an aching heart.

And then I realized how much my own failings
had cost my heavenly Father. I am older now—and
supposedly wiser—so when I fail, my loving Father's
heart aches on my account.

How can I not extend the
treasure of forgiveness to
others when God so richly
extends it to me?

Angela Elwell Hunt,
*Women of Faith
Devotional Bible*

GOD'S LOVE OVERFLOWS

*"'You shall love the LORD your God with all your heart,
with all your soul, with all your mind,
and with all your strength.' This is the first
commandment. And the second, like it, is this:
'You shall love your neighbor as yourself.'"*

MARK 12:30–31

The first commandment came after the first commitment. In the beginning God loved us first. When we understand His love for us, we don't have to be commanded to love Him; we simply respond to what He has already given. Secondly, we give away what we have been given. Everything flows from God loving the world first. We love Him in return and love others with the overflow of His love. Without God loving us first, there would be nothing to respond to, and there would be no overflow. He started it flowing down; we stand under the waterfall to receive and then share.

Nicole Johnson, *Women of Faith Devotional Bible*

TRY KINDNESS!

*Love your enemies, do good,
and lend, hoping for nothing in return.*

LUKE 6:35

The pattern of God's kindness to us is an example to follow. There is so little kindness in the world. Kindness is love in action. Kindness does someone good even when they don't deserve it.

Do you have a teenager who is bucking your every request? Try kindness. Are you a caregiver to a difficult elderly relative? Try being kind. Kindness wins the heart so you can speak to the mind. Kindness disarms the skeptic and convinces the agnostic there may be a good God after all. Try kindness!

Jill P. Briscoe, *Women of Faith Devotional Bible*

GOD BECAME MAN

*The Word became flesh and dwelt among us,
and we beheld His glory.*

JOHN 1:14

C. S. Lewis compared God becoming man to man becoming a toad for the sake of toads. Preposterous!

When God became man in the Person of Jesus Christ, it was the highest manifestation of grace the world has ever known. One who knew no sin, no sorrow, no frailty at all came to earth in human form to take our place as payment for all the sin of all mankind.

It would be hard for most of us to take anyone else's place in suffering. But He did it for you and me. Preposterous, extravagant grace!

Mary Graham, *Women of Faith Devotional Bible*

BEAUTY IN HIDDEN PLACES

Do not let your adornment be merely outward . . .
rather let it be the hidden person of the heart, with the
incorruptible beauty of a gentle and quiet spirit.

1 PETER 3:3–4

I prefer to suit myself in decorating my house, even if nobody else will ever see my creations. I have painted the insides of drawers in daring shades of green. I have color coordinated my laundry room. My prettiest birdfeeder is tucked away in the back yard, where even my neighbors cannot see it. It doesn't bother me that nobody sees my hidden treasures. I see them! Their beauty gives me joy.

How much more care should we take in putting the finishing touches on our hidden person—our soul? If you spend all your time decorating the outside of yourself, then you are just decorating for others. You are putting on a show, but all the while you are hiding dusty drawers and empty closets. Though nobody but God will ever see the hidden places of your heart, don't neglect that part. Beautify your hidden spots. And the results will be precious in the eyes of God.

Christa Kinde, *Living In Jesus*

WALKING BY FAITH

*It is God who arms me with strength,
and makes my way perfect.*

PSALM 18:32

Joshua gave the order to the priests at the edge
of the Jordan. He said, "Go to the water's
edge, put your feet in, and the people will cross to
the other side" (Joshua 3).

Think about the incredible faith it must have
taken for these priests to do that! They walked
over to the edge of the water, put their feet in,
and the minute the water touched the soles of
their feet, the water parted. Without flinching,
the priests walked into the middle of a now dry
riverbed, holding the ark of the covenant, until
two million people had crossed to the other side.

The priests, by faith, put their feet in the
water. Peter, by faith, got out of the boat and
walked toward Jesus. These were unnatural acts
according to nature. But with God, it was no
problem at all! Perhaps God is saying to you, "I
want you to believe Me, even on the edge of your
Jordan, and move ahead without fear."

Marilyn Meberg, *Overcoming Difficulties*

ALL THAT IS TRUE

Let us therefore come boldly to the throne of grace,
that we may obtain mercy
and find grace to help in time of need.

HEBREWS 4:14

You don't have to wait until your emotions are in check before you come to Jesus. He wants us to come as we are, broken and bruised with tear-stained faces. We bring together all that is true about us and all that is true about God.

We are invited to come right now as we are, ragged at the edges, splattered by the mud of life, invited into the very heart of heaven, and called to move close and approach the throne of grace. You don't have to tidy yourself up, clean up your own mess, or wait till you feel holy. Just come now into His presence. Jesus sees your pain and longs to comfort you. As my friend, Barbara Johnson says, "Let God wrap you in His comfort blanket of love."

Sheila Walsh,
The Heartache No One Sees

FRIENDS WITH GOD

*"No longer do I call you servants . . .
but I have called you friends."*

MATTHEW 15:15

Sometimes a mother can look into the face of her child and be struck to the very core of her being with love. The emotion is so intense it almost hurts with a sweet sting that brings tears to the eyes. Mother-love must be one of the strongest feelings possible. It can cause moms to do the strangest things!

Yet God loves us *more* than that. "In His goodness He chose to make us His own children by giving us His true Word. And we, out of all creation, became His choice possession" (James 1:18, NLT). He did some pretty wild things on our behalf, too. How astonishing to find the Master of the Universe taking time to build relationships with friends and disciples. "No longer do I call you servants . . . but I have called you friends." That hand of friendship has been extended to us as well!

Christa Kinde, *Discovering God's Will for Your Life*

"Constantly Abiding"

You, O LORD, are our Father;
our Redeemer from Everlasting is Your name.

ISAIAH 63:16

As a small child accompanying my dad to his tent-meeting revivals, I would sometimes sing that old hymn "Constantly Abiding" for the crowd. My dad would place a chair on the sawdust floor and lift me up on it so the audience could see me, a cute little girl wearing a bright red dress, white, lace stockings, black patent leather shoes, and a big bow holding back the bangs of my Buster Brown haircut. Then, as I sang, my dad would stand beside me, beaming proudly. Whether I was performing solo or with him, his arm was always around me, holding me securely as I stood on the chair and belted out the words.

Hearing the old hymns now instantly transports me back more than half a century to one of those tent meetings somewhere. I can smell the sawdust shavings on the floor and, best of all, remember the comfort of my dad's arm holding me secure.

Barbara Johnson, *Leaking Laffs*

ILLUMINE THE DARKNESS

While you have the light, believe in the light,
that you may become sons of light.

JOHN 12:36

With the Spirit of God in our hearts, we have the ability to reflect light—the light of Jesus Christ. He's the Source; we're the beams.

Think of it this way: When you were a child holding a mirror in your hand, if you caught a glint of the sun, that mirror reflected a beam that could actually illumine a dark place. That was pretty exciting! You had the power to shine in the darkness. It was better than holding a flashlight because the reflection source was from above you, not from batteries in your hand. It was supernatural phenomena to every child.

Each of God's children has the power to illumine the darkness. This light shows up in different forms: humor, kindness, peace, hope, grace—all characteristics that can come out of us when the light Source shines through us.

Luci Swindoll, *Women of Faith Devotional Bible*

GRACIOUS LOVE

*"A new commandment I give to you,
that you love one another; as I have loved you,
that you also love one another."*

JOHN 13:34

Have you noticed how you tend to save your most important words for your children or a close friend until just before you leave them—in hopes that this they will be sure to remember? That's exactly what Jesus did when He broke bread with His disciples on the evening before He died.

Of all the things He wanted them to remember, this was essential: that they love each other as He had loved them. God gives the world the right to judge whether or not we know Him at all by the love we have for each other. When all is said and done, that's what counts. Do we love each other in the gracious, longsuffering, courageous way God loves us?

Paula Rinehart, *Women of Faith Devotional Bible*

WHITER THAN SNOW

Wash me and I shall be whiter than snow. . . .
Create in me a clean heart, O God.

PSALM 51:7, 10

My husband recently came to me in our laundry room and handed me one of his favorite white shirts. I cringed at the blueberry stain he showed me, left from the pancakes he had enjoyed during a business breakfast. I went to work with every chemical I could find, washed the shirt three times, and finally breathed a sigh of stainless relief.

Forgiveness happens in much the same way. God loves it when we bring our stained garments to Him. He doesn't smack us around or stress out that perhaps the blemishes may not go away. Instead, as soon as we ask Him, the mess we've made is erased.

My husband smiled with gratitude when I handed him back his clean white shirt. You can accept the gift of forgiveness, too. The same God who forgave you and washed your garments white as snow can help you forgive others.

Lynda Hunter-Bjorklund, *Women of Faith Devotional Bible*

FORGIVENESS OFFERS GRACE

*There is therefore now no condemnation
for those who are in Christ Jesus, who do not walk
according to the flesh, but according to the Spirit.*

ROMANS 8:1

No condemnation? None? Zip? Zilch? Wow!
What a huge truth to get our arms around!
Human nature is full of condemnation. I still
remember the looks some adults gave me even as a
kid. At times I wasn't sure what I had done, but I
felt their piercing disapproval. And certainly there
were plenty of times I was blameworthy. My
naughtiness went clean to the bone.

As an adult, when I find myself severe in my
thoughts toward others who have offended me,
I remember Romans 8. Christ freed me from all
condemnation when He paid for my failures,
mistakes, and bone-deep
naughtiness, and His
forgiveness offers me the
grace and liberty to
forgive others. Whew!

Patsy Clairmont, *Women
of Faith Devotional Bible*

EVERLASTING LIFE

God so loved the world that He gave His only begotten
Son, that whoever believes in Him should not perish
but have everlasting life.

JOHN 3:16

I have known this verse since I was a child in
Sunday school. It is probably the first verse I
ever memorized. It's a verse full of life and meaning.

The Greek word used here for "everlasting"
refers not only to how long we live but also to the
quality of life we live right now, as contrasted
with a sense of hopelessness. Everlasting, or
eternal, life is a deepening and growing experience
every day. It can never be exhausted. It speaks of a
new quality of life. *We are not saved to simply*
make it through this world until we are finally
home free. Christ died to give us life, life right
now. Are you experiencing that? If, like me, you
are longing to be in relationship with the only
One who sees all our brokenness and longs to
bring healing and hope, may I remind you that
there is such a One? His name is Jesus.

Sheila Walsh, *The Heartache No One Sees*

GET YOUR HOPES UP!

*Now may the God of hope fill you with all joy
and peace in believing, that you may
abound in hope by the power of the Holy Spirit.*

ROMANS 15:13

A quotation that makes absolutely no sense to me is, "Don't get your hopes up." What! Why? The explanation to me was, "Well, if you get your hopes up and things don't work out like you want them, you'll be so disappointed." Whether you get your hopes up or not, there's still a chance for disappointment if things don't work out like you thought or planned. But come on! If your hopes don't go up, where are they going?

Hope is the confident expectancy that Jesus, the Peace Speaker, will bless us and empower us with God's qualities, so we can have more than enough of His peace in our hearts as we trust in Him.

Thelma Wells, *Women of
Faith Devotional Bible*

OUR REAL LIFE

Set your mind on things above,
not on things on the earth. For you died, and
your life is hidden with Christ in God.

COLOSSIANS 3:2–3

We talk about living—living dangerously, living large, living high, living it up. We claim a right to life. We work to make a living. Some of us live in the past, while others live for tomorrow. We live and learn. We live and let live. We have livable expectations. Our homes have lived-in looks. What more could we ask?

It's easy to get wrapped up in our day-to-day living. The world we live in is quite authentic—it is all we have ever known. But we forget this life is fleeting in comparison to the eternity that lies ahead. Paul says that our *real* life is hidden with God in Christ.

Christa Kinde, *Living In Jesus*

COMPELLING LOVE

Let all that you do be done with love.

1 CORINTHIANS 16:14

During my 105 days of incarceration in a Taliban prison, my father worked tirelessly to secure my release. Every day he talked with government officials, interviewed with countless reporters, and negotiated with members of the Taliban. As the situation in Afghanistan escalated, no one knew what our fate was to be or that of our many Afghan friends. Rumors floated across radio waves and television stations of possible execution or a years-long prison sentence.

Amidst all the chaos, my father announced his desire to take my place in prison and pay the penalty for the crime for which my friends and I were being accused. Knowing full well the potential severity of my sentence, my father loved me enough to give his life in exchange for my own. I did not deserve the gift he was willing to give or the sacrifice he was willing to make, but love compelled him to do whatever it took to set me free. So it is with the love of Christ.

Heather Mercer, *Women of Faith Devotional Bible*

SUFFERING HAS PURPOSE

We are hard-pressed on every side,
yet not crushed; we are perplexed, but not in despair.

2 CORINTHIANS 4:8

There is an enormous difference between perplexity and despair. When we're perplexed, we don't understand what everything means; when we're in despair, we decide that everything is meaningless. For us despair is an enemy like no other. It is osteoporosis of the spirit, stealing the nourishment of meaning from the suffering of life. As followers of Christ we trust that nothing is wasted, that even our suffering has purpose, but we stand against despair's claim that it has none.

Nicole Johnson, *Women of Faith Devotional Bible*

PROVIDER AND PROTECTOR

We walk by faith, not by sight.

2 CORINTHIANS 5:7

These seven little words describe an entire way of life. To operate in faith instead of what we see calls for an inner conviction that God can be trusted to do what He says. When our health is uncertain, He's our Physician. When we're down to our last dime, He's our Provider. When there's no energy, He's our Power. When the Enemy surrounds us, He's our Protector.

If we trust God to do what He says, then we have to trust His timing as well. This is hard for us planners. We prefer circumstances, people, and events to work on our timetable. This way we have the illusion we're in control!

God has to remind us all the time: *If I'm your Physician, Provider, Power, and Protector . . . don't you think you can trust Me to be your Planner as well?*

Luci Swindoll, *Women of Faith Devotional Bible*

A WORD TO LOVE

And let us not grow weary while doing good,
for in due season we shall reap if we do not lose heart.

GALATIANS 6:9

Hope is a word I love. Hope keeps you going when things don't look so good. Hope is the only thing left at times. I love it that God tells us not to lose hope. If we keep hope alive in our souls, we shall reap in due season. When we can't see past the darkness, we can always have hope. Isn't it great to know there are seasons to our lives? My season of life right now is raising three precious children under four years old—a great season, but a challenge every minute as well. I need hope that tomorrow may be easier or sweeter. "Thank You, Lord, for the hope You give me minute to minute."

Terry Jones (Point of Grace),
Women of Faith Devotional Bible

September

God's love is all we have
ever dreamed of.

PIECES OF OUR LIVES

Teach us to number our days,
that we may gain a heart of wisdom.

PSALM 90:12

Like a puzzle, every decision we make pops a little piece of our lives into place and establishes a pattern. For example, I decided to accept Ken Meberg's marriage proposal, and the result was a beautiful baby boy, Jeff Meberg. What if I had married Charlie Dillbean? There would never have been a Jeff—instead perhaps only a series of little Dillbeans whom I know I could not love like I love Jeff. And what about our adorable adopted daughter, Beth? If I hadn't chosen Ken as my mate, Beth would have been placed into some other couple's home.

It can be both encouraging and sobering to realize how our decisions influence our circumstances and help determine the level of contentedness we will experience in life. We have all made decisions we regret, decisions that have brought us pain. But we also have made decisions that were wise and for which we are grateful.

Marilyn Meberg, *Overcoming Difficulties*

GOD'S LOVE

The LORD raises those who are bowed down;
the LORD loves the righteous.

PSALM 146:8

Nothing can take God's love from us. I can say that of no other love. God pursues us, courts us, woos us to remind us. His love changes every day; it either intensifies, or my understanding of it grows, but I don't think it really matters which it is. He doesn't get tired of us, and He isn't frustrated by our moods or by our appearance. His love is all we have ever dreamed of. We are free to place the whole weight of our identity on Him. He will not lean, crumble, struggle, stagger, or falter in any way. His love is the answer to the questions of the culture. His embrace, the way to freedom. This love is why we were made.

Nicole Johnson, *Fresh-Brewed Life*

GOD WORKS MIRACLES

Is anything too hard for the LORD?

GENESIS 18:14

Sometimes God shows us His power in little ways. For instance—I am no a dog person. All that panting and drooling and whining and shedding—Yuck! But God can change even the most stubborn heart, and mine was softened towards the canine species to the point where I told my husband I wanted to get a puppy. In fact, when we came home from the breeder's house, we were the proud owners of two dogs—Chihuahuas! I named them Timothy and Titus.

That might not seem like much of a miracle to anybody else, but for our family, this was amazing. What are the miracles you might be seeking? Do you long for forgiveness towards someone who hurt you deeply? Perhaps you have a habit you long to break or a relationship that needs strengthening. No matter where you long to see newness and change, God can work in your heart to bring it to pass.

Christa Kinde, *Cultivating Contentment*

IT'S UP TO YOU

Whatever things are true, . . . whatever things
are of good report, . . . meditate on these things.

PHILIPPIANS 4:8

Peace is the result of choosing to focus your mind on what is true and honorable and right. When you choose to do that, it is amazing how much peace will overtake your mind and heart.

What you think about will determine how you feel. If you don't like how you feel, change your thinking. Circumstances rarely change, but *how you feel* about the circumstances can change dramatically as you alter the way you think. Your thoughts are not under the control of another person. You can hear what other people say, but you don't have to take their words into your mind and dwell on them. How you feel is up to you, not to anyone else in your life.

Jan Silvious, *Big Girls Don't Whine*

GRACE ALONE

For by grace you have been saved through faith,
and that not of yourselves; it is the gift of God,
not of works, lest anyone should boast.

EPHESIANS 2:8–9

Someone has said that grace is: **G**od's **R**iches
At **C**hrist's **E**xpense. Grace came to earth at
Christmas, opened a way to forgiveness at Easter,
and went to hell so that we needn't. Grace offers
us freely a home in heaven. Grace gives undeserving
people time and opportunity to find the reason
and purpose to life.

This grace cannot be bought with credit,
bargained for, or stolen. It matters not what color
or creed, class or religion you adhere to. You
cannot be good enough to merit it or bad enough
to be disqualified from receiving it. It can only be
found as we realize our lostness, mourn it, and ask
God to forgive us for Christ's sake.

"Grace alone" will offer us a way back to God.
Have you said thank you for God's riches at
Christ's expense?

Jill P. Briscoe, *Women of Faith Devotional Bible*

FORGIVE ONE ANOTHER

*Be kind to one another, tenderhearted,
forgiving one another, even as God in Christ forgave you.*

EPHESIANS 4:32

Here's an exercise: Each morning when you wake up, check the fertile soil of your heart to see if any bitter seed has taken root. That friend who betrayed you, the boss who berated you, the husband who barely understands you—bitter seeds will try to take root in every garden. Weeds are like that.

Next do this: For every bitter root that's come up, apply the greatest weed killer of all—forgiveness. To forgive is to cultivate a garden God will delight in, one filled with the flowers of kindness and tenderness.

Karen Kingsbury, *Women of Faith Devotional Bible*

EVERLASTING LOVE

*Walk in love, as Christ also has loved us
and given Himself for us.*

EPHESIANS 5:2

Every Wednesday afternoon at House of Hope, the teenagers and I have a cozy get-together which we call a fireside chat. The kids love to share from their hearts. Inevitably, they admit they have been looking for love in all the wrong places.

Most of these teens don't understand the true meaning of love. They have been brainwashed by TV, movies, magazines, and music that focuses on sex. As a result, they end up believing love is supposed to be self-satisfying rather than self*less*. They are left empty, hurt, and puzzled after spending money on seductive clothing, sensuous perfumes, feel-good drugs, and perverse one-night stands—all in a futile effort to fill the void inside.

Then they learn their "love tank" becomes full only when they experience the heart change that comes through knowing the love of Jesus Christ, which is free, satisfying, and everlasting.

Sara Trollinger, *Women of Faith Devotional Bible*

A Fulfilling Job

*Whatever you do in word or deed,
do all in the name of the Lord Jesus.*

COLOSSIANS 3:17

The Sunday morning service prior to "Labor Day" was jam packed with speeches dedicated to the encouragement of the domestic worker, governmental employee, labor union personnel, and everyone who worked outside the home.

As I think about this, I believe there should be more recognition of people who board buses, ride taxis, car pool, ride trains, commute from one city to another, travel in all kinds of weather, pay for childcare and flex their schedules to provide for their economic needs.

What I'm really saying is, "THANK YOU" my sisters for using your energy, enthusiasm, education, and enormous strength in the workplace, whether you are a wage earner or in that very important position of stay-home wife and mom. My prayer for you is whether you are an employer or an employee, your job would be fulfilling and worthy of all good things.

Thelma Wells, *WOF Association Letters*

UNSELFISH LOVE

Fulfill my joy by being like-minded,
having the same love, being of one accord.

PHILIPPIANS 2:1

The worst week of my life I found this scripture penned by my daughter, on a card she had left on her nightstand. She had died the preceding day unexpectedly. I was literally combing through her belongings, desperate for anything personal that had her mark on it. I took this card and kept it with her photographs and the many keepsakes she had saved over the years, almost as though she knew I'd need them someday.

We so often think of love as only reciprocal: If you love me, then I'll love you. But when we embrace the unselfish love of Christ and pass it on, we create a lifelong chronicle that will follow us into the next life. Even the broken parts of our lives become treasures to those we touch. What we leave behind here on earth becomes a kind of heavenly deposit into the hearts of those we esteemed higher than ourselves. Life is too brief to spend it in any other fashion.

Patricia Hickman, *Women of Faith Devotional Bible*

BEE Your Best!

I can do all things through Christ who strengthens me.

PHILIPPIANS 4:13

One of the messages God has allowed me to express is found in what I call "A Formula for Success": B + E + E = S, taken from my life's motto: "In Christ you can BEE your best!"

B means *Be aware of who you are.* You are a wonderful creation of God and there is nobody else like you.

E means *Eliminate the negatives in your life.* If you study your Bible, pray, praise God while you are hurting, and worship Him because He deserves it, you will refocus your attention from the negatives to the only One who can solve the situation.

E means *Expect the best from what you do, and let it all be for eternal value.* In whatever you do, ask, "Would Jesus approve of this?"

S means *Success.* Your success depends on putting God first, following the Scriptures, seeking the proper goals, persevering, and doing it all for Christ.

Thelma Wells, *Women of Faith Devotional Bible*

LOVED AS WE ARE

I have loved you with an everlasting love;
therefore with lovingkindness I have drawn you.

JEREMIAH 31:3

Here is the simple truth: God loves us passionately and intensely, and that love has nothing to do with the way we look. It isn't affected one ounce by the size of our blue jeans or the way our nose slopes up or how much dental work we've had done. It isn't lessened by wearing the wrong dress to a party or having no skill in applying makeup or by hating exercise. God simply loves us as we are. Which also means that if we get in shape or find a great hairstyle or learn to wear colors that look great on us, God still loves us—but He doesn't love us any more. We haven't "gone up" in His estimation of us. He loves us. Right now. Exactly where we are.

God is the One who has never criticized you or belittled you or made fun of your appearance in any way. He is the One who formed you, and said afterward, "This is good."

Nicole Johnson, *Fresh-Brewed Life*

WEEDS OF DISCONTENT

But you, . . . pursue righteousness,
godliness, faith, love, patience, gentleness.

1 TIMOTHY 6:11

My Dad has weeding down to a science. Starting in the spring, he'll till the ground, mark off the rows, and set up the fences. Then we'll go through and lay down newspaper that we've saved all winter long. Next comes a layer of straw. On top of that, we set out old tires in even rows. The tires are filled with soil and fertilizer from the neighbor's cow pasture. In these, we plant all our melons and squashes. Without any large areas of soil exposed, weeds don't take root. It's great!

When it's the soil of our hearts under cultivation, the crop we're hoping to reap is contentment. The efforts we put in early will prevent problems from cropping up later. A dependence on God as our only source of satisfaction, an attitude of thankfulness, and a trust that the Lord is working for our good—these keep the weeds of discontentment out of our lives.

Christa Kinde, *Cultivating Contentment*

FORGIVEN TO FORGIVE

As the elect of God, holy and beloved, put on tender mercies, kindness, humility, meekness, longsuffering; bearing with one another, and forgiving one another.

COLOSSIANS 3:12, 13

Evie was moving, and I helped her clean the apartment. Unfortunately her roommate had applied corkboard to the wall using the wrong adhesive, and it was impossible to remove. We picked, scraped, and scratched for hours.

Well into the process, I said, "You'd probably like to kill Janet about now." Evie replied, "No, not at all. After all Jesus has forgiven me, this is nothing."

Well. I knew that. Something about the way she said it, though, I've never forgotten. It's easier to forgive others when we put it in the context of what God's forgiven us.

Mary Graham,
Women of Faith Devotional Bible

PERFECT PEACE

You will keep him in perfect peace,
whose mind is stayed on You, because he trusts in You.

ISAIAH 26:3

Darlin', it's pretty clear that a lot of your worries are about what-if's. *What if something bad happens? How will I cope if a storm comes? If my world falls apart, will I?* Oh, what a vicious cycle that kind of worry and projection is!

Honey, if you keep telling yourself scary stories about all the scary things that might happen, you're going to get scared! Stop it! Take your thoughts captive in obedience to Christ, and choose to focus on how He's providing for you right here and now. God will keep in perfect peace the person whose mind is stayed on *Him.* Even if things aren't so purty for you in the present, He's still here, making sure that you have what you need to be okay. Paul assured us of that truth: "My God will meet all your needs according to his glorious riches in Christ Jesus" (Phil. 4:19 niv). Girl, that means *all!*

Thelma Wells, *Girl, Have I Got Good News for You*

THE PROCESS OF FORGIVING

*Be kind to one another, tenderhearted, forgiving one
another, even as God in Christ forgave you.*

EPHESIANS 4:32

Anger is the antithesis of joy. You hardly need
me to remind you that if you're full of angry
resentment, you will not be full of joy. The two
emotions cannot live together. Living with the byproducts of anger takes enormous energy. I don't
believe it is possible to expend energy for much
else. If that's the case, unless anger is neutralized,
joy and laughter will be rare experiences.

How do we begin the process of forgiving?
We begin where we are. If your resentment is still
so strong you don't really want to let go of it but
you know you should, acknowledge to God that
that is where you are. Then go one step further:
"I'm not willing to let go of my resentment, but
I'm willing to be made willing." God can then
begin to work to soften our spirit and to shape
our attitudes.

Marilyn Meberg, *Choosing the Amusing*

CARING FOR EACH OTHER

*May the Lord make you increase
and abound in love to one another and to all.*

1 THESSALONIANS 3:12

It was a privilege to grow up surrounded by my mother's friends. Because she had eight children she didn't go to places to visit. Her friends came to her, and I listened to their conversations.

Those wonderful women modeled a caring Christlike community. When anyone was sick or in trouble, or when there was a death in the family, my mother and her friends rallied to provide whatever was needed: a meal, a helping hand, a listening ear. They were a blessing in one another's lives. They demonstrated love, which through the years increased. Even today their influence shapes me.

Mary Graham,
Women of Faith Devotional Bible

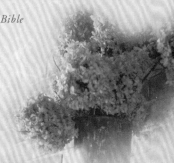

A Good Place to Start

Rejoice always, pray without ceasing,
in everything give things; for this is the will of God
in Christ Jesus for you.

1 THESSALONIANS 5:16–18

God's sovereign design for our lives is so far beyond our comprehension, the best thing we can do is take Him at His word and learn that thankfulness makes our days go better no matter what we face. He never said being grateful for something hard would be understandable or without heartache. He just said it was His will for us to do.

I've often been asked the question, "How do I know when I'm doing God's will?" While I can't answer that to the full satisfaction of the person asking, I can say this: Giving thanks in everything is a good place to start. In His sovereignty, God never makes a mistake.

Luci Swindoll, *Women of Faith Devotional Bible*

THE INVITATION

*"Come to Me, all you who labor and are heavy laden,
and I will give you rest."*

MATTHEW 11:28

"Come!" The invitation is always open to commune with God. No matter what. And the funny thing is that when we move an inch He'll move a mile. In those desperate times when we feel like we don't have an ounce of strength to "come," He will gently pick up our heads so that our eyes can behold something—something that will keep His hope alive in us. We are never without a source of hope. He will always come. Jesus will reach for you in ways that will break your heart. And if your heart cannot grasp it at the time—He will gently remind you of it later.

Kathy Troccoli,
Hope for a Woman's Heart

CONTENTIOUS OR PLEASANT?

*A continual dripping on a very rainy day
and a contentious woman are alike.*

PROVERBS 27:15

I have five of my Mom's paintings on my walls, but my favorite has to be in one called "Constant Drip." It's a painting of the faucet over the bathtub in the old farmhouse where I spent my childhood. It shows the old-fashioned knobs and a slightly cockeyed spout against white tile. The morning sun catches the glass bottles of bubble bath, and on the single drop of water that glistens on the verge of release. "Constant Drip" is the perfect title, because over the years, the tub has known the infrequent plinking of water.

Now the painting hangs over my bathtub and serves as a reminder to my heart of that verse in Proverbs: "A continual dripping on a very rainy day and a contentious woman are alike." It helps me think about my actions and attitudes. Am I making our house a place of welcome and peace, or am I a source of frustration and annoyance for those closest to me?

Christa Kinde, *Cultivating Contentment*

EVERYBODY WANTS PEACE

To be carnally minded is death,
but to be spiritually minded is life and peace.

ROMANS 8:6

Everybody wants peace, but there seems to be less peace in our world today than ever before. Peace is contagious. You possess it, and others are overwhelmed by it. As the peace of Christ consumes your life, it will influence your home. Your home will impact the street where you live. Your neighborhood will gain a reputation for being a great place to raise a family, impacting the entire community. All over the city, your community will be known as a peaceful place to live. Crime will decrease, and people will be able to walk the streets without fear.

Sound a bit idealistic? Why not give it a try and see what happens? Let the peace of Christ begin with you, and start to consume the world in which we live.

Babbie Mason, *Women of Faith*
Devotional Bible

FOCUS ON GOD'S POWER

*God has not given us a spirit of fear,
but of power and of love and of a sound mind.*

2 TIMOTHY 1:7

The quickest way to subtract is to add. Let me put it another way: If you move away from a best friend, the best way to fill the void is to make a new friend. If you have an "empty nest" at home, the best way to combat the blues is to find a new purpose.

It's the same with fear. To subtract it from your life, add a focus on the power of God in your life. Feel His love. Reason with the mind He gave you. These three can help you feel hope instead of fear about whatever situation you face.

Dianna Booher, *Women of Faith Devotional Bible*

Ring the Bells!

In Your presence is fullness of joy;
at Your right hand are pleasures forevermore.

PSALM 16:11

To me there's no more inspiring sound on earth than the heavenly *bonging* of the majestic bells that echo through the streets of small towns and cities everywhere, calling worshippers to church. And there's no more joyous noise than the cacophony of a tower full of church bells clanging away at the end of a worship service as the church doors are thrown open and Christians are released back into the world to spread the good news.

Maybe I love stories about bells so much because, frankly, I can identify with them. Bells can't help but be joyful, even when some people might not think it's appropriate. They just ring their hearts out, their uplifting tones merrily filling the air even when the situation would seem to call for a more restrained and dignified attitude. That's me!

Barbara Johnson, *Leaking Laffs*

THE CLASSROOM OF FAITH

Be diligent to present yourself approved to God,
a worker who does not need to be ashamed, rightly
dividing the word of truth.

2 TIMOTHY 2:15

When I was a middle-school music teacher, it was always fulfilling when I saw fruit for my labor. When students came to class, participated in the activities, studied hard, and did well on tests and even pop quizzes, it was a joy to give them a passing grade at the end of the semester.

Life's lessons are hard. You learn some lessons quickly. Others you find yourself repeating over and over again. But don't get discouraged. In the classroom of faith, you have the perfect Teacher available. God will help you with each and every assignment. He is very patient and will teach you everything you need to know. Listen and learn from Him. Remember the truth you have learned from Him. Then apply that truth to your life. You'll soon learn that when test time comes—and it will—the Teacher will rejoice in giving you a passing grade.

Babbie Mason, *Women of Faith Devotional Bible*

GOD'S WAY

My thoughts are not your thoughts,
nor are your ways My ways.

ISAIAH 55:8

As we ponder the big questions in life, our minds wander down well-worn paths. "Who am I?" "What should I do?" "Where should I go?" "Why am I here?" We long to do something of value, to be recognized, to distinguish ourselves, and to leave a legacy. As Christians, we also wish to discover God's will for our lives. Surely He is already laying the groundwork for our lofty aspirations in life. Then, when things don't quite meet our expectations, we are perturbed. And if they take a dire turn into disaster, we are perplexed. What went wrong? We missed the point.

The thing is, *God's* will is just that—God's will. He tends to do things His way, in His time, according to His plan, and with His purposes in mind. God often ignores our agenda! Over and over the Scriptures bring up an important theme: "My ways are not like your ways!" Sometimes we need a gentle reminder that He's not like us.

Christa Kinde, *Discovering God's Will for Your Life*

A BLESSED HOPE

*Let us hold fast the confession of our hope
without wavering, for He who promised is faithful.*

HEBREWS 10:23

The Greek word for *hope* means "to anticipate with pleasure; to expect or have confidence in." We find hope or confidence in the future by looking back at God's faithfulness in the past. Joshua did it in Joshua 12. He listed the 31 kingdoms his armies had already conquered. This recounting of past victories instilled hope in the people for the battles that lay ahead.

How sweet to lay hold of the same blessed hope for our futures because of what God has done in the past.

Lynda Hunter-Bjorklund,
Women of Faith Devotional Bible

SURPRISED BY JOY

The kingdom of God is not eating and drinking,
but righteousness and peace and joy in the Holy Spirit.

ROMANS 14:17

Joy catches us off guard. It is a response that wells up in our hearts from love. We can't control it, and we can't bring it about. We don't find joy; it finds us, often surprising us when it arrives—making us smile for no apparent reason, break into a tune when no one is around to hear it, or trust peacefully when things are falling down around our ears. Joy is never tied to wealth or circumstances or conditions, only love. A person who has every material possession might never experience joy, while someone who has nothing the world considers valuable may have joy like a rushing river. If you know love, you'll be surprised by joy.

Nicole Johnson, *Women of Faith Devotional Bible*

PURSUE JESUS THROUGH PRAYER

*Continue earnestly in prayer,
being vigilant in it with thanksgiving.*

COLOSSIANS 4:2

One of the most powerful ways of getting over the turmoil of the circumstances in your life is to fall madly in love with Jesus. How do you do that? Just like you pursue a man, you would pursue Jesus even more through prayer.

Prayer is the key that unlocks the door to God's heart. Saying The Lord's Prayer with meaning is one of the most powerful prayers you can pray. When you don't know what to say you can say, "Jesus!" Not as profanity, but in reverence to Him

You can read and listen to the Word of God and become absorbed in the Word. Just putting the Word in your mind will help you remember God's goodness and promises to you.

The result of all this is that you will develop a love for God that you didn't know you could have. You'll stop concentrating on past problems and begin to concentrate on the Problem Solver.

Thelma Wells, *WOF Association Letters*

THE THRONE OF GRACE

Let us therefore come boldly to the throne of grace,
that we may obtain mercy
and find grace to help in time of need.

HEBREWS 4:16

Every day in Afghanistan, dozens of widows and orphans approached us boldly on the street, begging for food, medicine, or money. Desperate and impoverished, these widows and orphans came to us for support. We loved and cared for them and always did our utmost to help, but often our resources were limited.

Like those widows and orphans, we are spiritual ragamuffins desperately in need of the grace and mercy of God. It is our lifeline, our spiritual food, an IV to our soul. Thankfully, the One who sits on the throne of grace possesses limitless resources, and He gives them freely; we need only come.

Heather Mercer,
Women of Faith Devotional Bible

GOD DOESN'T CHANGE

I am the LORD, I do not change.

MALACHI 3:6

I've lived by myself for the past thirty years, and it's been an interesting adventure. More often than not, there's been nobody in the wings to come to my aid financially, nobody to pick up the slack or run errands. Humanly speaking, all responsibility ultimately has fallen on me. Some days I feel OK about this; other days I don't—I feel overwhelmed. I can choose to let my overwhelming feelings guide my behavior (and sometimes I do), or I can choose to believe that God is with me and caring for me.

If I choose to live out of my emotions, no telling where I might go to salve my depression, dissatisfaction, or discouragement. Feelings fluctuate with the day, the wind, my hormones, circumstances, and human relationships. But because God told me He doesn't change, I can choose to believe Him no matter how I feel.

Luci Swindoll, *I Married Adventure*

LIFE IS SO . . . DAILY

*I have learned in whatever state I am, to be content: I
know how to be abased, and I know how to abound.*

PHILIPPIANS 4:11–12

Life *can* be so hard. Live can be so frustrating.
Life can be so . . . so . . . daily! Women
everywhere face disappointments, disarray,
downfalls, delays, drawbacks, and doldrums.
It's unavoidable. That's life! The trick is to face
life's twists and turns with grace. We yearn to be
the kind of women who exude contentment—that
quality of serene calmness. But that's so *hard* to do!

Contentment doesn't come naturally, and isn't
always learned quickly. But it can be learned. You
can, like Paul, say, "I have learned in whatever
state I am, to be content." With God's help we
can find satisfaction in daily living that cannot be
ruffled by circumstances. The key is
learning to trust that He is in
control of every situation and I
am in control of my response to
that situation.

Christa Kinde,
Cultivating Contentment

October

With Christ we always
have hope.

AN ANCHOR OF THE SOUL

This hope we have as an anchor of the soul,
both sure and steadfast, . . . even Jesus.

HEBREWS 6:19–20

After 9-11 some of my friends shared their fears and doubt with me. What might happen to America? What about the terrorist threats? Why would God allow such a thing to happen? Some people told me they felt tossed about by the waves of uncertainty.

I tried to answer those friends with truth from Scripture. All good things come from God, I told them. Therefore the attacks on America were not from God, but from the Evil One. Jesus told us the score straight up. In this life we will have trouble. But—don't miss this—God has already been victorious over this life. Victory comes in the shape of an old rough-hewn cross. In other words, God wins! Life may give us tough issues to face, difficult times, tests of faith. But with Christ we have hope like an anchor of the soul—sure and steadfast.

Karen Kingsbury, *Women of Faith Devotional Bible*

ATTITUDE IS EVERYTHING

Rejoice in the Lord always; again I will say, rejoice.

PHILIPPIANS 4:4

Attitude is everything and whatever is going on in life the way we respond is crucial. Paul is not being redundant when he says, "Rejoice, and again I say *rejoice.*" He effectively creates a picture for us. Imagine the sight of a little lamb coming out of the barn and jumping up once, then jumping up again. He leaps across the fields and hills, jumping as if for the sheer fun of it. So we are to rejoice and keep on rejoicing, not because things are wonderful, but because of the joy that comes from knowing the Lord is in the middle of things that are going on.

No matter how much you might want to be like Scarlet O'Hara and deal with life's realities *tomorrow,* that is no way to live. No matter your circumstances, rejoice and rejoice again, because God is the author and finisher of life. He is in the middle of everything you face, no matter what.

Jan Silvious, *Big Girls Don't Whine*

The Autumn of Life

To everything there is a season,
a time for every purpose under heaven.

ECCLESIASTES 3:1

Michigan really knows how to show off in autumn. Our maples scream reds, golds, and oranges, not to mention the riotous mums with their yellows and purples exploding throughout the landscape. The black-eyed Susans squeal with delight as pumpkins appear on porches.

Perhaps you like me are in the autumn of your life. Spring now seems a millennium away, summer has gone all too quickly, and suddenly like so many fallen leaves swirling at your ankles, autumn is upon you. The view from this season is quickly changing like a yellow and crimson maple leaf. We can shudder at the change or dance in the wind. Even though my joints squeak now, I choose to pirouette in my autumn, for winter is at the doorstep, and my season to sit by the fire nears. So watch out world—Patsy the swirling, twirling, joint aching, hot flashing, joy shouting woman is on the loose! Come join me!

Patsy Clairmont, *WOF Association Letters*

RUNNING A RACE

Let us run with endurance the race that is set before us.

HEBREWS 12:2

During high school, I ran track and cross-country. I trained three hours per day, performing sprints, running repeat miles, and lifting weights. My desire to run the best race possible affected what I ate and drank, how much I slept, and how I managed my time. When race day came, I was ready. Standing on the starting line, gun ready to fire, adrenaline pumping. I occasionally wondered, *Can I really do this?* Then I would look up and see the crowds and my teammates ready to cheer me on.

In Christ we've been called to run a race— a race to pursue His presence and His purposes. Sin keeps us from being able to run that race the way God intended. Christ, in his own hour of need, looked to the finish line of heaven with His eyes fixed on the reward of His suffering—His Bride— and was able to fulfill what He was sent to do. Let us follow His example.

Heather Mercer, *Women of Faith Devotional Bible*

LOVED BY GOD

*As the Father loved Me,
I also have loved you; abide in My love.*

JOHN 15:9

We are loved passionately by God. And I don't know why. It is a mystery, and it must remain a mystery. To understand it is to dismiss it as we are prone to dismiss every other love in our lives. If we discovered that God loved us because we were smart, then we would try to do everything we could to be smarter so He would love us more. If we met someone smarter than we are, we would fall into despair. We couldn't believe God would love us if we weren't the smartest. So I don't think God will ever let us know the reason that He loves us as passionately as He does. I don't have a clue why God loves me. But I believe in the core of my being that He does. So I surrender to it. I stop fighting it. I cease trying to figure it out. I collapse on it.

Nicole Johnson,
Fresh-Brewed Life

CHRIST REMAINS THE SAME

Jesus Christ is the same yesterday, today, and forever.

HEBREWS 13:8

We want things to remain the same. *Same* makes us feel safe. But the earth is in a constant state of movement. The wind blows and slowly breaks down the hillside. The rains shift the earth. The ocean tide rolls in and out.

Life changes. Our roles in life change. We are the youngest child, the little sister, or the artistic one. Soon, though, we are the dependable one that a child turns to in time of need. One day we are forced to become our parents' caregiver, and we are suddenly the stable one.

What on *earth* is the same yesterday, today, and forever? Nothing. Christ *in heaven* is the only thing that remains the same yesterday, today, and forever. He is the One to whom we look for care, the One we depend upon in times of need, the stable One. In uncertainty He is certain.

Kathy Troccoli, *Women of Faith Devotional Bible*

God Loves to Surprise

Keep me as the apple of Your eye;
hide me under the shadow of Your wings.

PSALM 17:8

Usually, when we pray, we know exactly what we want God to do. We've given our situation much thought, we've checked out the pros and cons, considered our options, and we've decided how God should work.

Unfortunately, God doesn't operate this way. I think he delights in surprising us. Just look at all the surprises He slipped into the Bible! Sarah had a baby when she was ninety-nine years old. Jacob was reunited with his son he thought had been killed by wild animals. The widow who shared the last bit of food in her house with Elijah found herself in possession of a pitcher that never ran out of oil. Improbable? Unbelievable? Incredible? Inconceivable? And yet, true.

Things don't always work out the way we think they should. That's because God has something better in mind.

Christa Kinde, *Adventurous Prayer*

MORE PRECIOUS THAN GOLD

In this you greatly rejoice . . . that the genuineness
of your faith, being much more precious
than gold that perishes, though it is tested by fire,
may be found to praise, honor, and glory.

1 PETER 1:6–7

When gold is refined, it is a fiery process that separates what is true from the flaws and impurities that have become one with it. The process is faithful, but it is temporary. We are called to more. We are impressed with gold and fine jewels, but God is blessed by faith that has come through fire hot enough to burn away what cannot last in His kingdom. At times we are so blistered by the blaze, it seems no good can come out of this fire. In those moments, we must hold on by faith to what we know is true. When we cling to Jesus at the height of the inferno, we will see when the furnace has cooled what is left is faith—pure, genuine, and honoring to Christ.

Sheila Walsh, *Women of Faith Devotional Bible*

RISE-UP TIME

In the morning my spirit longs for you.

ISAIAH 26:9

Although I don't *have* to get up at the crack of dawn, I enjoy doing just that. Those early morning hours are precious to me; they may be the closest thing to heaven I experience all day. The phone doesn't ring. There are no loud cars passing by on the street. No letter carriers or UPS deliverers are ringing the doorbell. The day's crises have not managed to intrude. When someone sent me a list of early-risers in the Bible, I was cheered by the thought that the time of day I love so much has always been a special time for God's children:

Abraham got up early and "returned to the place where he stood before the Lord."

Moses climbed Mount Sinai early in the morning to meet God.

Job's "regular" custom was to worship God "early in the morning."

The psalmist wrote, "In the morning, O LORD, you hear my voice" (Ps. 5:3).

Barbara Johnson, *Leaking Laffs*

HOPE IN GOD

*Always be ready to give a defense to everyone
who asks you a reason for the hope that is in you,
with meekness and fear.*

1 PETER 3:15

I'll never forget the time I prayed about whether
or not we could adopt a child. In His
unmistakable voice, the Lord gave me Proverbs
13:12 as a promise: "When the desire comes, it is
a tree of life." Not if, but when! I rested in the
hope that God would send us the right child at
the right time.

A friend later asked me how I could have
such confident hope. "I don't know if my faith is
that big," she said.

"The size of my faith doesn't matter," I
answered. "I'm confident in the size of my God."

Angela Elwell Hunt, *Women of Faith Devotional Bible*

A Bundle of Emotions

*Beloved, let us love one another, for love is of God;
and everyone who loves is born of God and knows God.*

1 JOHN 4:7

Some days, our feelings seem out of control.
We're just reacting to everything that lands in
front of us, and we feel like we just can't help it.

It might seem as if our moods and emotions
are a curse rather than a blessing. They give us so
much trouble! What good are moods if they only
make us crazy? What good are emotions if they
only confuse us? But God has given women all
these emotions for a very good reason. Think about
it. Women are more empathetic. We are able to put
ourselves in another's place and understand
instinctively how someone else is feeling. We cry
easily because we feel for one another. Women are
capable of great understanding, great compassion,
and great mercy. When Jesus urged His followers to
love one another, care for one another, and
encourage one another, He gave women a
commission for which they were perfectly suited!

Christa Kinde, *Managing Your Moods*

INESTIMABLE WORTH

A new commandment I give to you,
that you love one another; as I have loved you,
that you also love one another.

JOHN 13:34

Just as Jesus first considered the worth of the person, so must we. Though someone's performance may displease us, our role is not to judge, alienate, or condemn. The cleansing of sin and the modification of behavior is God's job. Recognizing the inestimable worth of each of God's children is ours.

As we consider our role in loving one another rather than judging one another, we need to remember there is a vast difference between acceptance and approval. We are not mandated to approve of wrong behavior. Jesus did not approve of the adulterous behavior of the woman at the well, but He did accept her as one worthy of His love and provision.

Marilyn Meberg,
Choosing the Amusing

SAY YOU'RE SORRY

If we confess our sins, He is faithful and just to forgive us our sins and to cleanse us from all unrighteousness.

1 JOHN 1:9

When we misbehaved, my mother would say to us, "Say you're sorry." I never knew why that was important. I rarely felt sorry.

Now when I become aware of sin—actions or attitudes that aren't according to God's Word—I agree with Him that I'm in the wrong, acknowledge His forgiveness, and move on.

He deals with all sin the same way. He deals with all people who sin the same way.

He died for everybody's sin. All sin. We experience the freedom of His forgiveness when we stand in agreement with Him. It's like saying we're sorry. The Bible calls it confessing.

Mary Graham, *Women of Faith Devotional Bible*

WISDOM IS LEARNED

If any of you lacks wisdom, let him ask of God,
who gives to all liberally . . . and it will be given to him.

JAMES 1:5

We live and survive by *wisdom,* a gift that always requires us to choose one thing over another. We can choose to be wise or we can choose to be foolish. (The consequences, however, are not ours to choose.) And unlike instinct, wisdom is learned. We have to learn what we must do to be wise, then make the choice to embrace what we have *learned,* and ultimately practice it as a way of life. This is the journey we take from immaturity to maturity.

Immaturity longs to be older, wiser, bigger, and more in control; maturity is *being* older, wiser, bigger and more in control. Immaturity is impulsive choices based on emotional reactions; maturity is thoughtful, sound choices. Hands down, maturity is the preferred state.

Jan Silvious, *Big Girls Don't Whine*

GOD'S LAVISH LOVE

Behold what manner of love the Father has bestowed on us, that we should be called children of God!

1 JOHN 3:1

God loves the unloved and the unlovely. He loves us when we hate Him. He loves us when we ignore or are indifferent to Him. That's what the love of God is like. It is primarily concerned with the others' well-being despite negative reaction or response.

"Like Father, like son," so they say. The children should take after the Father.

Do we love others as we have been loved of God? Do we love the unlovely and lavish love on those who ignore us, hate us, and despise us? The Holy Spirit will scatter such love around our lives if only we will ask Him.

Jill P. Briscoe, *Women of Faith Devotional Bible*

GOOD GIFTS

*Having then gifts differing according
to the grace that is given to us, let us use them.*

ROMANS 12:6

I have heard that the only people who should attempt to write poetry are those who cannot *not* write poetry.

What about you? Can you not help but hug people? Can you not help but notice the emotions that people are trying desperately to hide? Can you not help but bake? Can you not help but draw, write letters, grow African violets, cuddle babies, make things look pretty, sing, read, organize, play piano, fix things, straighten pictures, take the lead, adopt stray animals, get someone to laugh? God has gifted each of us uniquely with something we cannot help but do. What have you been given? Perfect pitch, an eye for color, a way with numbers, a knack for getting people to work together, a love for children, a recipe for a mean bowl of chili, a heart for animals. It may seem small, but given to God, it can accomplish much for His kingdom.

Christa Kinde, *Adventurous Prayer*

A Thankful Heart

Enter into His gates with thanksgiving,
and into His courts with praise.

PSALM 100:4

Do you know the difference between *joy* and *happiness?* Happiness depends on what is happening around us. But true joy just bubbles up from inside and is constant regardless of our circumstances.

One way to develop the joyful habit is to nurture an attitude of thankfulness. As someone said, God has two dwelling places—one in heaven and the other in a thankful heart. When God dwells in our thankful hearts we can't be anything but joyful. Science confirms that truth. After years of studying people with joyful temperaments, one researcher concluded, "The first secret is gratitude. All happy people are grateful. Ungrateful people cannot be happy."

Barbara Johnson, *Leaking Laffs*

WALKING IN TRUTH

*I rejoiced greatly that I have found
some of your children walking in truth,
as we received commandment from the Father.*

2 JOHN 4

"If she tells you something you can take it to the bank" is a common saying meant to convey that a person's word counts. They don't brag; they don't lie, they don't hedge. It's the truth and nothing but the truth.

Can you imagine having that standard applied to everything in your life—your words, actions, motives, and thoughts! "Walking in truth" encompasses living every standard God has set before us: loving as He loved, showing compassion as He showed compassion, meeting needs as He did, praying as He prayed.

"Walking in truth" means getting your head out of the clouds and off the pillow so you can be alert to what God's teaching you in every situation and how He wants to use you each day. It's movement with a passion and a purpose.

Dianna Booher, *Women of Faith Devotional Bible*

YOUR TRUE VALUE

My soul, wait silently for God alone,
for my expectation is from Him.

PSALM 62:5

Your true value is not about the person you married or didn't marry. It is not about how good you are at what you do. It is really just about one thing: your relationship to God. Have you made the decision to allow Him to call the shots? Have you decided to listen to Him and let Him comfort your soul? Have you accepted the fact that your life is in His hands and that He will enable you to do everything you need to do?

If you can't say that yet, it's okay. You can start living that way today. Simply tell yourself, whatever is going on, "This is not about me. This is really all about Christ and His power to strengthen me and to get me through this day." That truth will get you through any stage of life, whether single or attached whether young or old, whether sick or well. Christ is committed to you and longs for you to be committed to Him.

Jan Silvious, *Big Girls Don't Whine*

Everyday Praise

I will bless the LORD at all times,
His praise shall continually be in my mouth.

PSALM 34:1

We know all about everyday things. We have everyday clothes—our "grungies" we wear when we clean house, join the kids in the sand box, and mow the lawn. We have everyday shoes—well worn, and comfy. We have everyday hairstyles—wash and wear, no fuss, no muss. We have everyday dishes—dishwasher safe and durable.

But when we're getting ready to go out, or when we're having company, that's when we get out the good stuff. We take out the dry-clean-only dresses, spend time in front of a mirror on our hair, slip into a pair of leather pumps, and lay out the fine china.

God is not a " special occasion." You don't have to get into your Sunday best, drive to the nearest sanctuary, and be led by a worship team in order to praise God. Giving God glory is something that happens every day. God wants to be part of your normal, everyday routine.

Christa Kinde, *A Life of Worship*

A Rich, Strong Life

*In this you greatly rejoice, though now
for a little while, if need be, you have been
grieved by various trials.*

1 PETER 1:6

The darker the roast of the coffee, the more intense the flavor. It stands to reason that for a rich, strong life, we are going to have to go through the fire. This "roasting" can deepen our walk. The finer the grind of the beans, the more concentrated the coffee. First Peter 1:3 tells us that in His great mercy, God has given us new birth into a "living hope," through Jesus. That's the identity we now have. We are children of God, and our hope is alive. "In this you greatly rejoice, though now for a little while you may have had to suffer grief in all kinds of trials." These trials have come, the Scripture says, "so that your faith—of greater worth than gold, which perishes even though refined by fire—may be proved genuine" (1 Pet. 1:6–7, NIV). This genuine, refined by fire, holding-on-for-dear-life faith will result in praise and glory to Christ.

Nicole Johnson, *Fresh-Brewed Life*

318 WOMEN OF FAITH

An Exalted Position

*To Him who loved us and washed us from our sins
in His own blood, and has made us kings
and priests to His God and Father, to Him be glory
and dominion forever and ever.*

REVELATION 1:5–6

As I meditate on this powerful greeting John gives to the seven churches, I find that I must fall on my knees in praise and adoration of our Lord. Christ's love cannot be doubted. He sacrificed His sinless life in order to cleanse us from our sinfulness. He who is the King of kings and our great High Priest graces us with dignity by exalting us to the position of kings and priests.

And what should be our response to such love? A life lived in holiness, in kingly victory over the world, and in consecrated service to the One whose love is without end. To Him be the glory!

Cynthia Heald,
Women of Faith Devotional Bible

THE SOURCE OF JOY

Hope in God; for I shall yet praise Him,
the help of my countenance and my God.

PSALM 43:5

Our hope is indeed in God, the source of our joy. If we are not experiencing joy, perhaps David's prayer in Psalm 51:12 could be ours: "Restore to me the joy of Your salvation, and uphold me by Your generous spirit." Our salvation is Jesus; because of Him, we anticipate an everlasting eternity with the God of the universe. Before that eternity is ours, however, we live out our days on this earth. We want to live them with joy. We want to live them with health.

God has given to each of us an incomparable medicine bag—in it is the divinely created ability to laugh at ourselves, at our circumstances, at humor produced by others, and to take a less threatened view of everything around us. To utilize the contents of that bag is to experience healing for our minds, our souls, and our bodies.

Marilyn Meberg, *Choosing the Amusing*

CENTERED ON CHRIST

The law was given through Moses,
but grace and truth came through Jesus Christ.

JOHN 1:16

Jesus reflects the perfect balance between knowing the truth and living from the heart. Jesus has neither a sterile, academic approach to life, nor an undue emphasis on emotionalism. He brings together our heads and our hearts to make us soulish persons who reflect the harmony of grace and truth, just as He did when He was on this earth.

So many people are fragmented. Their lives are broken and splintered. They don't know who they are and can't figure out why they're here. Their lives contain very little joy and no sense of adventure. But what Christ offers us, today and every day of our lives, is just the opposite. We're given wholeness because we are centered on Him who is the center of the universe. Through prayer, we have constant communion with Him. Christ is our solid center, our absolute Monarch, and in Him we think and move and feel and have our being.

Luci Swindoll, *I Married Adventure*

NO MORE TEARS

God will wipe away every tear from their eyes.

REVELATION 7:17

I'm a stoic when it comes to vaccinations. No cringing. No whimpering. No fainting. I'm fine as long as I don't have to look at the needle. Nobody likes to get shots, but we're resigned to the fact that they serve their purpose. Besides, they're over pretty quickly.

Someday our lives here on earth will be just like that little pricking sting. A dim memory. A faint recollection. Over. All the troubles and discomforts of our days here will fade into the distance once eternity is in view. We will no longer be consumed by mortgage payments, grocery bills, job security, or calorie counting. There will be no more pain. No more stubbed toes, migraine headaches.

Our bodies will be made new. Our souls will find perfect peace. And God will wipe away every tear.

Christa Kinde, *Women of Faith Devotional Bible*

Not Safe, but Good

"My thoughts are not your thoughts,
nor are your ways My ways," says the LORD.

ISAIAH 55:8

In C. S . Lewis's classic book *The Lion, the Witch and the Wardrobe,* four children are evacuated from London to the English countryside during World War II. Lucy, the youngest child, discovers the magical world of Narnia that's accessible through a wardrobe in a spare room. At first her brothers and sister refuse to believe there is such a place until they, too, pass through the wardrobe to the world hidden behind a rack of fur coats. There they find the wicked Snow Queen and the magnificent Aslan. In this tale, the lion Aslan represents Christ. The children are overwhelmed by this majestic animal and want to know if he is safe. "Oh no," they are told. "He is not safe, but he is good!"

That's just it though; God's not safe in the sense that we have Him in a box, predictable and measured. Just when we think we have a handle on His ways, God does something we never expected.

Sheila Walsh, *Outrageous Love*

PRAYER CHANGES THINGS

The entrance of Your words gives light;
it gives understanding.

PSALM 119:130

Prayer has been one of he sweetest adventures of my life. I believe with all my heart that prayer really does change things.

Prayer also changes me. As I praise God, my burdens lift. The burdens themselves may not change, but they're transferred from my shoulders to God's. As I unload my cares on Him, I sense His presence and strengthening. As I confess my sin and wrong attitudes, I know He forgives me. Since He lives in me, geographically that transfer is done in a matter of seconds—if I can just remember that.

Luci Swindoll, *I Married Adventure*

OUR GREAT WEDDING DAY

If I go and prepare a place for you,
I will come again and receive you to Myself;
that where I am, there you may be also.

JOHN 14:3

The Jewish wedding ceremony took place in three parts. It began with the "betrothal," which was preceded by intense bargaining between the father of the bride and the father of the groom. When the bride price was paid, there was a ceremony in which the couple was "betrothed." Next, the groom went away in order to add a room to his father's house for his bride. During this time of separation, the bride was preparing her wedding gown.

The price Jesus paid for us was not silver or gold but His precious blood. If we have put our trust in that blood, there is a ring on our finger. We are betrothed. Our bridegroom has gone away, but He will be back. As we anticipate our great wedding day, we are preparing our "wedding gown." Rather than fine linens, our wedding gown is the purity of our character.

Dee Brestin and Kathy Troccoli, *The Colors of His Love*

GOD WROTE THE BOOK!

All Scripture is given by inspiration of God.

2 TIMOTHY 3:16

I can't prove the Bible to be true. There are, however, many convincing reasons to believe it to be true. To cite a few, is it not interesting that this Book has inspired the highest level of moral living known to humankind? And isn't it also interesting that this Book speaks of a Christ who is admired and quoted even by skeptics? Another fact about the Bible that gives it credibility is that it is made up of sixty-six books that evolved over a period of fifteen centuries. It was written in three different languages by forty different human authors ranging from kings to fishermen. All those authors with centuries between their writings are in total agreement as they describe who God is and what His purpose is. They didn't have the luxury of checking each other's stories to make sure they were writing the same thing.

How does one account for that total unity of theme and message? Quite simply, it's because *God wrote the Book!*

Marilyn Meberg, *Overcoming Difficulties*

BELOVED OF GOD

The LORD God is my strength;
He will make my feet like deer's feet, and He will
make me walk on my high hills.

HABAKKUK 3:19

As Christians, we are the beloved of God. We can stake our claim on that promised land. We can choose to trust it and allow it to change us, or we can mistrust it. Not trusting it doesn't make it any less true. It simply makes it untrue for us. It keeps us locked out of the freedom of experiencing God's embrace. It's like being invited to a party and mistrusting the invitation. The party is going on with or without us. Should we choose not to attend, we are the ones who lose.

Understanding who we are in Christ intellectually will not change us unless we trust that identity in the core of our being. We are completely and totally loved and embraced in the arms of God.

Nicole Johnson,
Fresh-Brewed Life

OUR SERVANT KING

Through love serve one another.

GALATIANS 5:13

If we were royal heirs to an earthly monarch, we might have grand, attention-getting duties such as leading military campaigns or reigning over lavish ceremonial affairs. Instead, we are heirs to a servant King, whom we honor by serving others in humility and in love. Our responsibilities may not be glorious deeds that win us loud acclaim—at least not on this side of heaven. Here, our tasks may be something much simpler—and even more important:

> To speak a healing word to a broken heart.
> To extend a hand to one who has fallen.
> To give a smile to those whose laughter has
>   been lost.
> To light the candle of God's word in the
>   midst of another's darkest night.

Barbara Johnson, *Leaking Laffs*

November

When we call out God's name,
we have His undivided attention.

ROBED IN RIGHTEOUSNESS

Let us therefore come boldly to the throne of grace,
that we may obtain mercy
and find grace to help in time of need.

HEBREWS 4:16

One sweet lady I know looks like a watercolor painting—soft blue eyes, porcelain skin, blond hair that's almost white. Everything she loves would have to have the word "light," "pale," "soft," or "icy" put in front of its color. Then there's this guy I went to college with. He wore such vividly colored shirts that they easily earned the adjective loud. Before they were ever stylish, he was wearing colors that made people squint. He had the most outrageous taste. But his style suited his outgoing personality and quirky sense of humor.

Whatever your color preference might be, Jesus has invited you to come into the hush of His Father's throne room with all the boldness of a loud shirt. He won't be startled. You are there at His Son's invitation. And whether you're wearing icy pink or tangerine, He sees you robed in righteousness.

Christa Kinde, *Adventurous Prayer*

OUTRAGEOUS LOVE

Love suffers long and is kind.

1 CORINTHIANS 13:4

Every night when I tuck my son into bed I ask him this question, "Which boy does Mommy love?"

He will put his hand on his cheek and reply, "This boy!"

May I suggest that every time you catch your reflection in a mirror you ask yourself this question? "Which girl does Jesus love?"

Put your hand on your cheek and say with absolute confidence, "This girl!"

One of the greatest struggles that we will face on this earth is forgiving those who have wounded us. We can't do it on our own, but God's outrageous love teaches us how to forgive. It is God's gift to us to help us live in a world that is not fair.

Sheila Walsh,
Outrageous Love

WAITING PATIENTLY

*Call to Me, and I will answer you, and show you
great and mighty things, which you do not know.*

JEREMIAH 33:3

Sometimes it's hard to explain hope—just
what is hope, anyway? The cutest illustration
of hope I've found is about a little boy who was
standing at the foot of the escalator in a big
department store, intently watching the handrail.
He never took his eyes off the handrail as the
escalator kept going around and around. A
salesperson saw him and finally asked him if he
was lost. The little fellow replied, "Nope. I'm just
waiting for my chewing gum to come back."

If your face is in the dust, if you are in a
wringer situation, be like the little boy waiting for
his chewing gum to come back. Stand firm, be
patient, and trust God. Then get busy with your
life . . . there is work to do.

Barbara Johnson,
*Stick a Geranium in Your
Hat and Be Happy*

THE LANGUAGE OF LOVE

"This is My commandment,
that you love one another as I have loved you."

JOHN 15:12

We show God's love to each other in relationship. When we forgive each other, that is a sign of God's forgiveness of us. We are never more like God than when we forgive others. Relationships afford us our greatest opportunity to model the gospel. We are called to be light-bearers in a dark world that only recognizes one language: love. The Scripture tells us that the world will only recognize us as followers of Christ by the love that we have for one another.

There is nothing more powerful than seeing a couple who love each other working side by side to communicate that love to the world. This communication happens far more by what they do than by what they say. To stand together with another individual in love—with one mission, purpose, and passion—speaks volumes.

Nicole Johnson, *Fresh-Brewed Life*

FUN AND LAUGHTER

The joy of the LORD is your strength.

NEHEMIAH 8:12

I believe we all have the capacity for fun and laughter. We do not all have the same abilities in creating humor—we are not all stand-up comics, but we can all laugh.

You may feel there are times in life that simply will not yield even an ounce of humor. May I suggest that during those seemingly interminable times of pain, you fight to see beyond the restrictive confines of the immediate; remind yourself that those moments will not last forever. Whatever it is that threatens to crush your spirit and claim your joy today will not necessarily be there tomorrow, next month, or next year. Life moves forward and circumstances change. You will not always be in a pit. That reminder in itself brings a respite to the soul.

Marilyn Meberg,
Choosing the Amusing

THE BIBLE ENDURES

Blessed are those who keep His testimonies,
who seek Him with the whole heart.

PSALM 119:2

The Bible is an amazing volume of work—like no other! In sixty-six books there is perfect historical continuity from the creation of the world to the new heaven and the new earth. This collection of authors—kings, peasants, philosophers, physicians, fishermen, statesmen, poets, and plowmen—couldn't have known much about each other because they lived in various countries, and their writings extended over sixty generations of human history, representing sixteen hundred years . . . yet it all fits together. The book is a phenomenon without question, and it is utterly inexhaustible.

Voltaire, the French infidel who died in 1778, predicted the Bible would be obsolete within a hundred years, but here we are in the twenty-first century proving him wrong. The Bible endures. And not only does it endure; its truth continues to transform lives.

Luci Swindoll, *I Married Adventure*

NOVEMBER 7

SUFFICIENT IN CHRIST

I can do all things through Christ who strengthens me.

PHILIPPIANS 4:13

Charlie and I raised three boys. Whenever I had to run to the doctor with busted chins or fingers that had been slammed in car doors or hands that had fishhooks stuck in them, he was never there. That wasn't by design by design but by circumstance. Charlie was often on military duty or working out of town, and he just wasn't available. It always fell to me to get the boys to the ER by myself.

Through all those years, I learned the secret of being self-sufficient in Christ. That is, I learned that I could do what needed to be done and be what I needed to be *because I had Christ living in me giving me the strength and wisdom I needed to get the job done.* Once that is settled in your own mind and you are firmly convinced that it is true, you can turn your heart and head toward living life as a woman who does her job well.

Jan Silvious, *Big Girls Don't Whine*

336 WOMEN OF FAITH

"CALL TO ME"

*Call to Me, and I will answer you, and show you
great and mighty things, which you do not know.*

JEREMIAH 33:3

John says the only reason we love God is because He first loved us. In the same way, we could not pray to our Heavenly Father if He had not first asked us to do so. "Call to me," invites our Heavenly Father. It is an invitation to pray. He has made Himself available to us 24/7/365. He has put out the welcome mat. He has given us the green light. We have a direct line to His throne room. We have a permission slip, a backstage pass, an engraved invitation. He has an open door policy for all of His children. And when we do call out His name, He gives us His undivided attention.

Christa Kinde, *Adventurous Prayer*

LAUGHING AT YOURSELF

*A merry heart does good, like medicine,
but a broken spirit dries the bones.*

PROVERBS 17:22

It's healthy to be willing to laugh at yourself and make light of your shortcomings. We all have our quirks, so we shouldn't take ourselves too seriously. One of the best solutions I know for that is to take the "bunnyslipper approach," a philosophy of life we all need to practice.

A friend sent me a pair of bunny slippers, and every now and then I put them on, especially when I'm tempted to start thinking I'm important or "nearly famous." There's something about bunny slippers that keeps my perspective where it belongs, but in addition to that, my bunny slippers remind me that whatever happens doesn't have to get me down. I can still be a little silly and laugh and enjoy life. Pain dissolves, frustrations vanish, and burdens roll away when I have on my bunny slippers.

Barbara Johnson, *Mama,
Get the Hammer!*

SET FREE

Let us draw near to God with
a true heart in full assurance of faith.

HEBREWS 10:22

We lose our way. We want hope. We want forgiveness. We want restoration. We want freedom.

We must continually take trips to the cross. We must live a life of repentance. We must keep our hands open so that God can fill them. He will forgive. He will restore. He will set free. We can be different than what life "sets us up to be."

Hebrews 10:22 says: "Let us draw near to God with a true heart in full assurance of faith, having our hearts sprinkled from an evil conscience and our bodies washed with pure water." God's worthiness flows into our unworthiness and we become worthy. If we want the Lord to empower us we must come under His rule. His commands are for us and not against us. They are not to constrain us but to free us.

Kathy Troccoli, *Hope for a Woman's Heart*

GOD ANSWERS PRAYER

*And whatever you ask in My name, that I will do,
that the Father may be glorified in the Son.*

JOHN 14:13

Robert Moffat, missionary to south Africa, returned to recruit helpers in his Scottish homeland. Arriving at the church where he was to speak, he was disturbed to note that only a small group of ladies had braved the elements to hear his message based on, *"Unto you, O men, I call"* (Prov. 8:4). Moffat felt hopeless as he gave the appeal, realizing that few women could be expected to undergo the rigorous experiences of the jungles. But God works in mysterious ways to carry out His wise purposes.

Moffat failed to notice one boy in the loft who had come to work the bellows of the organ. This young fellow was thrilled by Moffat's challenge. Deciding that he would follow in the footsteps of this pioneer missionary, he went to school, obtained a degree in medicine, and spent the rest of his life ministering to the unreached tribes of Africa. His name: Dr. David Livingston!

Lana Bateman, *The Heart of Prayer*

SERVE ONE ANOTHER

Through love serve one another.

GALATIANS 5:13

From time to time, we give in to the fact that it's time to do a little spring cleaning. With a wide range of cleaning supplies, we tackle the dirt and the grime that finds its way into our homes. Scouring sinks, changing bedding, doing dishes, loading the washing machine, mopping floors, dusting furniture, polishing windows, and shaking out rugs. It wouldn't be so bad if we had a little help! At some point, we want to throw down or dustpan and throw up our hands, and cry out, "I'm not the cleaning woman you know!" We sometimes feel like slaves to our tasks.

But aren't we? Jesus was willing to do a slave's job by washing His disciples' feet. And when He was done, He told His disciples they should serve one another too. Jesus didn't say we would always be appreciated. He didn't say we'd never be taken for granted. What He asks of us is to love and to serve. What better place to practice than in our own home?

Christa Kinde, *Encouraging One Another*

MY LINK TO SANITY!

Wait on the LORD; be of good courage,
and He shall strengthen your heart.

PSALM 27:14

Prayer is my link to sanity, stability, and longevity. Am I suggesting we live longer when we pray? Possibly. There's nothing like quiet reflective moments to encourage our blood pressures to stop percolating, our hearts to fall back into rhythm, and our minds to stop gyrating. Then add to all of that the untold benefits of loving exchanges with our all-knowing, all-seeing, all-powerful God. He who assigns our days and redeems our losses has a way of calming our anxieties and even healing our infirmities.

I love that the Lord is not only hospitable but He is invitational. That's probably why He is said to be "The Door." Jesus makes our entrance to the Father possible. He knew we would need time in His presence where we could step out of the whirlwind and into His consoling company. It is there, as we lean our heads upon His breast, that we are both deeply heard and deeply understood.

Patsy Clairmont, *Adventurous Prayer*

ONE OF A KIND

*I will praise You, for I am fearfully
and wonderfully made; marvelous are Your works.*

PSALM 139:14

There is something exhilarating about variety. Don't you love to see a garden of flowers aglow with myriad colors, shapes, and sizes? The garden would lose much of its appeal if it were all one species, one color, and one shape. Can you imagine a symphony performed only by tubas? We need some tubas, but we need cellos, violins, French horns, clarinets, and so forth for a rich, full sound. By the same token, I think we achieve a full, rich sound in life when there is variety among us; when our uniqueness is encouraged so that we make a different sound or look from that of everyone around us.

The inevitable result of rigid conformity is a lack of personal authenticity—a phony rather than real approach to ourselves, to others, and to life's experiences. God did not create any duplicates in nature or humankind.

Marilyn Meberg, *Choosing the Amusing*

FRIENDSHIP AND TRUTH

As iron sharpens iron so one man sharpens another.

PROVERBS 27:17

What a great verse. It came to mind not long ago when I was sharpening a knife in the kitchen. I'd been trying to slice a tomato and had almost hacked the thing to mush. Finally, it hit my numb skull that the knife needed a good sharpening. Duh. I took out a whetstone and had at it. In no time it was a razor, slicing that tomato beautifully. Metal met metal, and what was dull and ineffective was once again functioning at high efficiency.

That's friendship whetted by truth. Without a willingness to recognize our own shortcomings, value correction, or set about changing and growing up, friendship will simply die. Of dullness! It will have no value.

Luci Swindoll,
I Married Adventure

LOOKING FOR LAUGHTER

Happy are the people whose God is LORD!

PSALM 144:5

We can learn to look for laughter and joy in the many ordinary places where we go. When I go to our La Habra post office in the morning, the cement on the sidewalk outside is just plain blah gray. But if I go in the afternoon, when the sun hits it, the cement sparkles with a million transient diamonds! So, I usually go in the afternoon, looking for the joy that can bounce off that cement right into my life, to remind me of the sparkles all around us, if we are willing to look for them.

But I repeat, you have to LOOK for the joy. Look for the light of God that is hitting your life, and you will find sparkles you didn't know were there.

Barbara Johnson,
Stick a Geranium in Your Hat and Be Happy

STANDING OUT IN THE CROWD

By this all will know that you are My disciples,
if you have love one for another.

JOHN 13:35

The year the new VW Bug came out, my mother-in-law bought one. Aren't they just the cutest little cars? Hers is black, and she keeps the little bud vase in the dashboard stocked with a spray of pink roses—her signature flower. She named the car Sophia. My children all know that Grandma drives a black bug, and even a one-year-old can distinguish a VW Bug from the other cars in traffic. Everywhere we go, from the freeways to back ways, the kids pick them out—red ones, yellow ones, blue ones, and lime green ones. And invariably they will sing out "I see a Bug! Is it Grandma?"

Jesus told us that, because of our love for others, we would be easy to pick out in this world—just like a VW Bug is easy to spot on the freeway. We'll stand out because we're different. Do you stand out in the crowd?

Christa Kinde, *Encouraging One Another*

WE CAN COUNT ON HIM

Jesus Christ is the same yesterday, today, and forever.

HEBREWS 13:8

God is eternal, infinite, sovereign, omnipotent, omniscient, omnipresent, and immutable. In addition, He is perfect love, grace, patience, and compassion. He's holy, righteous, just, and faithful. God is all of these things every day, all the time, and I can count on it because it says so in the Bible, and I believe the Bible to be absolutely true.

In my lifetime, I've seen thousands of fads come and go, philosophies of life change like the weather, political systems overturned in revolutions. Nothing stays steady. Except God! The essence of His being is always the same: yesterday, today, and forever. We can trust Him and His Word. If we live to be 110, . . . we can count on Him.

Luci Swindoll,
I Married Adventure

INSPIRED BY SELFLESSNESS

*As we have opportunity, let us do good to all,
especially to those who are of the household of faith.*

GALATIANS 6:10

A few years ago at the Seattle Special Olympics, nine contestants assembled at the starting line for the on-hundred-yard dash, with a relish to run the race to the finish and win. All, that is, except one boy who stumbled on the asphalt, tumbled over a couple of times, and began to cry. When the other eight contestants heard the boy cry, they slowed down and looked back. Then they all turned around and went back to where he'd fallen. Every one of them. One girl with Down syndrome bent down, kissed him, and said, "This will make it better." Then all nine children linked arms and walked across the finish line together. Everyone in the stadium stood and cheered.

We are touched and inspired by their behavior because their most elemental instinct was to rise up as a unit to tend to the well-being of their competitor. We love to see their lack of concern for winning and see instead their commitment to caring.

Marilyn Meberg, *The Zippered Heart*

TREASURES IN HEAVEN

Do not lay up for yourselves treasures on earth, . . .
but lay up for yourselves treasures in heaven.

MATTHEW 6:19

When we talk of storing our "treasures" in heaven rather than on earth, we know we are talking about two different kinds of treasures. The thing we'll cherish most in heaven won't be a *thing* at all. It will be living in the presence of our loving Father and Creator. In fact, our palaces in heaven probably won't need any closets. After all, we're not going to bring any earthly treasures along with us.

In heaven we won't be encumbered by all the material goods that clutter our lives here on earth. Whatever their size our heavenly homes will be places of love set in neighborhoods where the peace is never interrupted. How comforting to know we'll share it with our friends and loved ones who are waiting for us there.

Barbara Johnson,
Leaking Laffs

PARENTS PARTNER WITH GOD

She made a vow and said, "O LORD of hosts, if You . . . will give Your maidservant a male child, then I will give him to the LORD all the days of his life."

1 SAMUEL 1:11

Hannah longed for a son more than anything else in the world. She persisted in asking God for a son and made a vow that the child would be given back to God. Within a year she gave birth to Samuel. She cradled him in her arms and remembered her vow. It's hard to imagine wanting a baby as badly as Hannah did and then knowing she would have to give him up one day soon. But she kept her word without wavering. When Samuel was weaned, she took him to live with Eli the priest. She knew that Samuel belonged to the Lord.

I know plenty of moms who worry bout sending their children out into the world, but that is what God asks us to do, isn't it? Because parenting is not about us, it's about partnering with God to prepare our kids to do His work.

Jan Silvious, *Big Girls Don't Whine*

Unseen and Secret

"When you pray, go into your room, close the door and pray to your Father, who is unseen. Then your Father, who sees what is done in secret, will reward you."

MATTHEW 6:6, (NIV)

There are two key words in that verse: *unseen* and *secret.* This is what Jesus asks us to do. Pray to our Father who is unseen, who sees what is done in secret. These words are mentioned clearly. Jesus works through and in the unseen and the secret. Sometimes we wish He would hold a press conference and explain what He is doing. We want to understand clearly and know immediately. It is just in our nature. But it is not in His nature to do so. Look at how He handled His own deity. He didn't walk around with a sign on His back that said,

I AM THE SON OF GOD!

He just was. He just is.

Kathy Troccoli,
Hope for a Woman's Heart

A PLACE OF REST

*May the God of peace . . . make you complete
in every good work to do His will, working in you
what is well pleasing in His sight.*

HEBREWS 13:20–21

When we see that He controls all things, every situation is an opportunity to look for what God has invested in that moment or in that struggle.

No more do we ask ourselves, "Why did I do something so ridiculous?" But rather, we turn to our Father and say, "You allowed this. What are You trying to show me, Lord . . . what are You trying to teach me . . . what do I need to see?"

Understanding God's sovereignty can make prayer a place of rest. No matter what we ask, He abides over us and our prayers. A sovereign God reigns and longs to teach us to pray the desires of His heart even within the desires of our own.

Lana Bateman,
The Heart of Prayer

CHILDREN OF THE KING

*You did not receive the spirit of bondage again to fear,
but you received the Spirit of adoption.*

ROMANS 8:15

The average apology for the shame-based person is, "Excuse me for living." Does anyone deserve to feel that way? Absolutely not! When we understand that those shame messages are not deserved—that they are, in fact, lies—we can grab the biggest shovel we can find and start digging, rooting out, and discarding. Yahoo!

God sent His Son, Jesus, to be for us what we could never be: perfect. As a result, in the eyes of God the Father we have priceless value! Shame has no right to lodge within us or dictate who we are. Messages that undermine, criticize, and demean have no basis in fact. The fact is that we are children of the King!

Marilyn Meberg, *The Zippered Heart*

A SENSE OF HUMOR

A merry heart does good, like medicine,
but a broken spirit dries the bones.

PROVERBS 17:22

According to my birth certificate, I am living somewhere between estrogen and death, or, as someone said, between menopause and LARGE PRINT! But I don't have to act my age because, thank God, I've discovered a wonder anti-aging remedy. It won't actually turn back the clock, and it's certainly not a new wonder drug. In fact, it's been promoted since biblical times as a cure for a wide variety of problems (see Proverbs 17:22). And it's no secret, either; lots of people use it. (They're the ones I'd like to take my next cruise trip with!)

If you know anything about me, or if you've read any of books, you can already guess what I'm talking about. It's the same God-given gift that's kept me functioning through some previous tragedies.

What is it? Laughter. A sense of humor.

Barbara Johnson,
Living Somewhere Between Estrogen and Death

STRENGTH AND BEAUTY

*Every branch that bears fruit He prunes,
that it may bear more fruit.*

JOHN 15:2

One of my favorite flowers is an annual called cosmos. They have very tall stems, often bringing their blooms and more than four feet into the air. The first few years I put them in garden, I was tremendously disappointed. They grew, but the plants were tall and spindly, often having only one or two flowers.

I had never known that my precious plants needed pinching. While a young plant is just starting out, a gardener must come along and nip the top right off the plant. In response, the plant sends out two new branches to grow upwards from the broken spot.

Sometimes God has to do a little pruning in our lives. There are things we must let go. There are events that force us to branch out in unexpected ways. Even when these changes pinch a little, God's purpose is for our good—strength and beauty in our souls.

Christa Kinde, *Encouraging One Another*

GOD HOLDS THE FUTURE

"I know the plans I have for you," declares the LORD,
"plans to prosper you and not to harm you."

JEREMIAH 29:11

Because I believe God has a plan for my life, both temporally and eternally, I want to live in a way that will please Him. I may not always know what that is, but I generally know what it's not. It's my responsibility to strike out in faith, believing He will show me as I go along. God holds the future of my life. I feel secure in the fact that the blood of His Son was shed for my sins and because of that fact I will spend eternity in heaven. With this as a given, I want my activities on earth to count for Him. I what to invest time in active fellowship with Jesus, because I believe that the closer I am to God the better my life will be, even in its worst moments.

Luci Swindoll, *I Married Adventure*

SPECIAL COMFORT

You have been grieved by various trials, that the genuineness of your faith, . . . may be found to praise, honor, and glory at the revelation of Jesus Christ.

1 PETER 1:6–7

First Peter 1:6 is a special comfort when you are in the middle of a crisis. It was penned by the apostle Peter, who was writing to people whose lives were in one big upheaval. They were Christians under Roman rule who were daily confronted with the possibility of a crisis, like being snatched off the street and hung on a lamppost to burn for being a Christian. They lived in terrifying times, and the trials were horrific. So imagine the comfort when Peter wrote, "In this [speaking of the salvation they had been given] you greatly rejoice, even though now for a little while, if necessary, you have been grieved by various trials." In the original translation, that phrase "for a little while," is "how little, how little." Your crisis may seem long, but compared to eternity, you know it has a limit. It will not last forever. Every crisis has a beginning and an end.

Jan Silvious, *Big Girls Don't Whine*

FORMED BY GOD

Before I formed you in the womb I knew you.

JEREMIAH 1:5

A child in Harriet Beecher Stowe's *Uncle Tom's Cabin* was asked, "Do you know who made you?" She speculated, "Nobody, as I knows on," said the child with a short laugh. "I 'spect I jist grow'd."

But the Bible says something very different. One of my favorite verses in Scripture is Jeremiah 1:5: "Before I formed you in the womb I knew you." That is a mind-boggling thought. Before I was ever in the womb of my mother, I was in the mind of my sovereign Creator. What does that mean? God apparently mused, pondered, and thought about my essence and my identity before He called me into being. I am not a composite of haphazardly thrown-together molecules, traits, and characteristics.

We are persons of great complexity and enormous potential, thoughtfully and deliberately formed by the Almighty. We are not creations who "jist grow'd."

Marilyn Meberg, *The Zippered Heart*

HOLD ON TO CHRIST

*When you pass through the waters, I will be with you;
and through the rivers, they shall not overflow you.
When you walk through the fire, you shall not be
burned, nor shall the flame scorch you.*

ISAIAH 43:2

I love this verse from Isaiah. It makes it clear that at times we will walk through difficult places that we would never have chosen for ourselves, but we will not be alone.

That is quite a promise. It doesn't say that we won't pass through the waters; it says that Christ will be with us. It doesn't tell us that rivers won't roar at our feet; it says that they will not overwhelm us. There will be fiery places, but because of God's great love, we will not be consumed. Hold on to that promise when your feet are wet and the smell of smoke is in your hair. Hold on to Christ, for He is holding on to you.

Sheila Walsh,
The Heartache No One Sees

December

*We are never without
the life of God.
We are never without hope.*

ENCOURAGEMENT FOR FAITH

*But you, beloved, building yourselves up
on your most holy faith, praying in the Holy Spirit,
keep yourselves in the love of God.*

JUDE 20, 21

What kinds of things make you feel happy? Advertisers know! Why else would television commercials be filled with beautiful landscapes, spring flowers, clean sheets, cuddly puppies. These images can really tug at your heartstrings. Admit it—you've actually cried over some of those old Hallmark commercials! We are easily influenced and even manipulated by our emotions.

We mostly think of encouragement as being a mood-lifter. It's that little compliment, a bouquet of flowers, an unexpected present, or a warm hug. But the encouragement God provides touches us more deeply than that. He doesn't offer a quick fix when our feelings are frazzled. What He's offering us is encouragement for our faith. If we are strong in the faith department, we are less likely to let our emotions drag us down.

Christa Kinde, *Encouraging One Another*

DO SOMETHING OUTRAGEOUS!

Happy are the people whose God is the LORD!

PSALM 144:15

How long has it been since YOU did something outrageous? How long has it been since you ate watermelon and tried to see how far you could spit the seeds? Or gathered big armfuls of lilacs and brought them to friends so their homes would smell like spring? Or marched in a parade or climbed up the down escalator?

Did you ever watch a child swat madly at specks of dust hanging suspended in a shaft of sunlight? Children delight at such innocent, simple things—and so can you. Become a child again. Laugh! It's like jogging on the inside. Look for ways to enjoy your day—however small or trivial—even finding a convenient parking space! Look at a field of flowers and see FLOWERS, not WEEDS!

Barbara Johnson, *Living Somewhere Between Estrogen and Death*

OUR RESPONSES

A man has joy by the answer of his mouth,
and a word spoken in due season, how good it is!

PROVERBS 15:23

Most of us assume that we would be loving, pleasant citizens if it were not for all those people and events that destroy our tranquillity and cause our heads to begin swelling. We think, *"If it weren't for . . . I'd be . . ."* But deep down we know that blaming others for how we feel or act is a cowardly bit of scapegoating that solves nothing. It just perpetuates the problem of being continually ticked off. So what's the answer?

To begin with, we have to take responsibility for our behavior and not blame others. That means that even though the insipid blonde bank teller is wildly annoying, our responses are under our control. We have a choice. We can offer the person arsenic tea . . or a courteous word and a smile.

Marilyn Meberg,
The Zippered Heart

SONGS OF OUR HEARTS

Sing to Him, sing psalms to Him;
talk of all His wondrous works!

1 CHRONICLES 16:9

Many years ago an old monk lived in a monastery in Europe. He sang the *Ave Maria* every Christmas Eve as the brothers celebrated the birth of Jesus. He had a poor voice and poor pitch, but no one wanted to take the honor away from him.

The old monk died shortly before Christmas one year, and a new young brother was asked to sing the traditional song. He was a highly gifted man who had been trained with the opera before taking his vows. A magnificent sound filled the abbey as the young monk began to sing.

Shortly after midnight, it was said that an angel visited the abbot. "Why was there no song to the Christ Child tonight?" he asked. "No song!" responded the abbot. "Never has there been a more beautiful song sung to our Lord than what was performed this night." "No," said the angel, "the Father reads the heart, and there was no song for the Christ Child this year."

Lana Bateman, *The Heart of Prayer*

FAITH FOR A LIFETIME 365

GOD TRULY CARES

Cast all your anxiety on him because he cares for you.

1 PETER 5:7, NIV

At the moment we cast our anxiety on our heavenly Father, believing He'll listen, understand, care, and act on our behalf, our burden is lifted. Believing He truly cares is worth a fortune in hope, victory, and spiritual rest. And knowing He is able to respond to our need is a comfort beyond all measure. I know He can do anything, and I feel safe and carefully tended, knowing He will accomplish what concerns me. These precious truths are in my head, and they've become priceless treasures buried deeply in my heart.

Luci Swindoll, *I Married Adventure*

THE LIFE INSIDE

*If our earthly house, this tent, is destroyed,
we have a building from God, a house not made
with hands, eternal in the heavens.*

2 CORINTHIANS 5:1

Take a picture of a healthy tree in the prime season of summer. The brilliance of the colors can be breathtaking. There is vibrancy. There is growth. There is life. Look at the same tree in the height of fall. Empty. Stripped. Alive on the inside, but dead on the outside.

How true it is for us as God's children. In this life our flesh may be dying, our circumstances may leave us feeling stripped of our pride or dignity, and our lives may seem empty of any promise. But the Spirit that raised Jesus from the dead lives inside of us! We are never without the life of God. We are never without hope. It is always within our grasp. We are never without the certainty of His promises. They are always there for us to build our lives upon.

Kathy Troccoli, *Hope for a Woman's Heart*

GOD OVER ALL THINGS

The LORD is great and greatly to be praised;
He is to be feared above all gods.

PSALM 96:4

In 1994 Dr. Frank Seekins wrote a book called *Hebrew Word Pictures*. In his book Dr. Seekins speaks of the fact that every Hebrew word has a definition, and that each letter in a Hebrew word is also a word picture and has a definition. By defining each letter within the word, and taking into consideration the root of the word, a phrase is produced that further clarifies the meaning of the word.

For instance, if we take the word *fear* in Hebrew, *Yearah,* and define each letter, considering the root of the word, we find the phrase, *to see the hand of.* In other words, to fear God we need to see the hand of God in all things—His sovereignty.

The Lord our God is not only God *of* all things, but God *over* all things.

Lana Bateman, *The Heart of Prayer*

THE PICTURE OF LIFE

My ears had heard of you before,
but now my eyes have seen you.

JOB 42:5, NCV

There is something about pain that repaints the picture of life. Of who we are, of who God is. I've said it myself. I look at my life. I think of the death of my father. I think of my struggle with clinical depression and that bleak winter of my soul, but even though I would not have chosen this path, I would not change a single day, a single step.

Why? Because I am a different woman. It's one thing to say that the Lord is my shepherd; it's quite something else to be unable to walk one more step by yourself, to lean on that staff, and to be held up. It's just as Job said, "My ears had heard of you before, but now my eyes have seen you" (Job 42:5, NCV).

Sheila Walsh, *Life Is Tough*
but God Is Faithful

ACCEPTED BY GOD

There is no fear in love; but perfect love casts out fear.

1 JOHN 4:18

In loving ourselves unconditionally as God does, we love and accept ourselves based, not on what we do, but on who we are. Many of us feel we can perhaps love ourselves if we do something well, if our performance is good. But how can we love ourselves when we make mistakes and do embarrassing things? That's the whole point; that's the shame-buster element. But if we love ourselves unconditionally, then even when we blow it badly, making huge or small mistakes, we do not waver in our agreement with God that we are still lovable—because He says we are!

I'm certainly not suggesting we ignore our mistakes and refuse to take responsibility for them. At the same time, while we learn to practice our "game," we continue to love ourselves no matter how many golf balls we send crashing through the windows of the house located too close the sixth tee.

Marilyn Meberg, *The Zippered Heart*

THE TAPESTRY OF LIFE

Yet in all these things we are more than conquerors through Him who loved us.

ROMANS 8:37

My life has included sorrow as well as happiness. And all those emotions, all those bitter-sweet memories, have created what I like to think of as a bright colorful, firmly woven tapestry. The happy times are the golden threads that catch the sunlight, warming the soul. The bright pattern was created by our children and then the grandchildren, whose sparkling threads added a nubby texture, a splash of vivid color, to the fabric. The black, somber woof threads that subdue the tapestry's gaudiness were painstakingly woven as we endured hardships in life.

As I reminisce, I think how my husband and I wove our way through joys and sorrow, good times and bad, glorying in each other's triumphs and supporting each other in times of trial. And in every loop and knot of our lives together, I see the hand of God.

Barbara Johnson,
Living Somewhere Between Estrogen and Death

SPIRITUAL CONFETTI

[I want] their hearts [to] be encouraged,
being knit together in love.

COLOSSIANS 2:2

Who doesn't love throwing confetti up in the air? At weddings, or parties or on New Year's Eve, everyone wants something in their hands to throw. It's a way of lavishing our love on people. Whether it's paper, rice, or birdseed, it's a way of cheering others on. Confetti is a tangible expression of our intangible emotions. Like happiness you can see and throw someone's way.

Encouragement is to a relationship what confetti is to a party. It's light, refreshing, and fun. It's cheer you can throw someone's way. But even deeper, it is the assurance you are there, that you are standing behind them and supporting them. The time it takes to gather little pieces of love, grace, strength, and hope is well worth it when you see what happens as you shower those gifts on someone else. It's like spiritual confetti, and it's the ultimate encouragement.

Nicole Johnson, *Encouraging One Another*

A HEAVENLY HOPE CHEST

Lay up for yourselves treasures in heaven,
where neither moth nor rust destroys
and where thieves do not break in and steal.

MATTHEW 6:20

Did you have a hope chest when you were a teenager? They were all the rage several decades ago. Every girl had one. Hope chests were a throwback to the days when a girl must have a dowry in order to marry. In more recent times, they were more of a practicality. As a girl learned the skills of sewing and homemaking, she began to set aside certain items for her hope chest. Embroidered pillowcases, lace doilies, quilts, rugs. No bride came empty-handed into her new home. Even before she was engaged to be married, she was laying aside little treasures that she would use later.

In a way, heaven is our hope chest, for we can lay aside treasures there, where they cannot be destroyed. Are you making preparations for eternity? Is your treasure in heaven?

Christa Kinde, *Living In Jesus*

God Came to Us

*Christ heals the brokenhearted
and binds up their wounds.*

PSALM 147:3:

When Jesus came, He came in a way that no one expected. He came to do what no one else could do. He came to bring healing that no one else could bring. He came to you and to me. He came to fulfill the promise of Psalm 147:3: *Christ heals the brokenhearted and binds up their wounds.* That is His commitment to us.

So many missed Him the night He was born. They were so close, but so far away, like someone who has sat in church for fifty years and never gotten the point. You can be inches away from the Christ and still miss the gift. You can be a very religious person and never receive the hope and healing offered through the sacrifice that Jesus made. You can stand staring up at the sky, crying out, "Does anyone in this cold, cruel world see me?" Jesus stepped into all the horror and betrayal of our world to answer our cries for help.

Sheila Walsh, *The Heartache No One Sees*

DEAD TO SIN

But you are not in the flesh but in the Spirit,
if indeed the Spirit of God dwells in you.

ROMANS 8:8–9

Here's the liberating truth: The sinning Christian is not evil! There is something evil within the Christian person that is doing the sinning, but the sin nature was killed and buried.

Admittedly, this is a very difficult truth to grasp. Perhaps this illustration will help. Although I had my silicone breast implants removed last year, my body still has toxic poison creeping sluggishly through its system. I know the silicone is there because I can see it on a sonogram and I can feel its effects in my body. But the reality is there is nothing wrong with me . . . I am a redeemed and valuable child of God. There is, however, something wrong in me, wrong in my body. I will feel the effects of what is wrong in my body until the day I die. The same is true of sin in me. I will always feel its presence and pull, but I am not that sin; I am a reborn child of God who is dead to sin.

Marilyn Meberg, *The Zippered Heart*

NEVER APART FROM GOD

*Neither death nor life, . . . nor height nor depth,
nor any other created thing,
shall be able to separate us from the love of God.*

ROMANS 8:38–39

S ome of the greatest words Paul ever wrote
start with questions: Can anything separate
us from the love Christ has for us? Can troubles
or problems or sufferings? If we have no food or
clothes, if we are in danger, or even if death
comes, can any of these things separate us from
Christ's love?

Paul's answer is that nothing—*absolutely
nothing*—in this entire world can separate us from
the love of God that is in Christ Jesus our Lord.
"For I am persuaded," Paul said, "that neither
death nor life, nor angels nor principalities, nor
things present nor things to come, nor height nor
depth, nor any other created thing, shall be able
to separate us from the love of God."

What an overwhelming statement! No matter
what happens, Jesus is enough.

Sheila Walsh, *Life Is Tough but God Is Faithful*

Surpassing Understanding

*The peace of God, which surpasses all understanding,
will guard your hearts and minds through Christ Jesus.*

PHILIPPIANS 4:7

I am seeing more clearly these days. My eyesight
is getting worse, but my spiritual sight is getting
better. It all makes a little more sense to me now.
I don't always have to "understand" to have His
peace. God's peace surpasses understanding. Isn't
that what it means in Philippians 4:7 when it talks
about a peace that transcends understanding? I know
that God is using the very things in my life that
caused me intense suffering to bring incredible
comfort. When I sing, when I speak, His healing
virtue is pouring through my wounds. Even now
in the places where I am still broken, God shines
His glory through my holes.

He'll use us in our weakness, and
we will see His strength.

Kathy Troccoli,
Hope for a Woman's Heart

LIVING IN THE PRESENT

Walk worthy of the calling with which you were called.

EPHESIANS 4:1

Moments come and go so fast, but they are what make up the whole of life. Little bitty moments here and there. They turn into hours and days and weeks—ultimately an entire lifetime. . . .

Life is short and everything is irrevocable. No matter what we do to lengthen the moment, we can't. No matter how eager we are to shorten uncomfortable events, that can't be done either. If we don't learn to live fully in the present, much of life passes us by, lost in the cobwebs of time forever. The passage of time can't be retrieved except in our memory banks. That's why we must be all there at any given moment. Even during the times that are frightening or difficult. Everything has a purpose, and if we don't want to miss that purpose and the adventure along the way, then we must be conscious, alert, curious, open-hearted. When we capture the moment we're in, we're fully alive.

Luci Swindoll, *I Married Adventure*

WORSHIP WITH YOUR LIFE

*God is Spirit, and those who worship
Him must worship in spirit and truth.*

JOHN 4:24

A few years ago I was given a note written by
Elaine Cook, a dear Bible teacher who lives
in British Columbia, Canada. Elaine had gone to
the Lord in her personal prayer time, asking Him
to teach her how to worship Him *with her life*. As
He began to impress her heart with His answer to
that prayer, she wrote these words:

*When you accept whatever situation you are in
without murmuring, you are worshipping Me.*

*When you can rejoice in Me in the midst of
your infirmities, you are worshipping Me.*

*When you look with compassion upon one who
is afflicted, tossed, and broken, then am I worshipped.*

*When you recognize My Body and
honor them as My brethren,
this is true worship unto Me.*

Lana Bateman,
The Heart of Prayer

A FORMULA FOR LAUGHTER

As he thinks in his heart, so is he.

PROVERBS 23:7

I don't usually respond to formulas for this and that; they feel a bit too tidy. But I have developed one for cheerful thinking I'd like to toss your way for consideration. To begin with, I love to laugh. I believe a giggle is always loitering about even in the most devastating of circumstances. I make a point of shuffling through the rubble in search of that giggle.

This isn't denial. I need to feel and express my pain. But I also need to find the light side—and there is *always* a light side! I've noticed that when I laugh about some minor part of a problem or controversy or worry, the whole situation suddenly seems much less negative to me. After a good laugh, I can then rethink my circumstances. As a result, that which was threatening may now seem less threatening.

Marilyn Meberg,
I'd Rather Be Laughing

GOD'S MIGHTY MESSENGERS

Do not be afraid, for behold, I bring you good tidings of great joy which will be to all people.

LUKE 2:10

What did the shepherds understand that Bethlehem night? We'll never know. Very few human eyes have seen the sky fit to burst with the presence of angels.

It's interesting that every time an angel addresses a man or woman, he has to start by saying, "Don't be afraid!" Angels must be spectacular to look at. Angels are very much part of the life of the believer. I don't think we even begin to take in the power that is around us every day. The birth of Christ was not the mild-mannered depiction we see on our Christmas cards every year. It was an invasion of all that is holy and good into everything that is corrupt and evil, a divine covert operation to set us free. In the guise of an innocent child, all of heaven was waging war with the enemy of our souls.

Sheila Walsh, *The Heartache No One Sees*

PLAYFUL PLEASURES

*"Unless you change and become like little children,
you will never enter the kingdom of heaven."*

MATTHEW 18:3, NIV

Our inner child wants to dawdle, putter, explore, enjoy, and make up things. It doesn't matter if they are pretty things or formed correctly. What matters is the pleasure that comes as the result of our creative efforts.

With the onslaught of life's demands and duties, some of us forget to be playful. We keep our inner child hidden, "proper" and in line, and we forget that it is she who can provide the enjoyment we long for in daily life. Pablo Picasso put it wisely: "Every child is an artist. The problem is how to remain an artist once that child grows up." Ah yes! There's the rub.

Don't be afraid to explore playful pleasures in your life. Let them spill outside the bounds of your leisure and work. Let them permeate your life. And the next time somebody asks for a volunteer to be a clown at the block party, raise your hand.

Luci Swindoll, *The Great Adventure*

"CHILL OUT"

*He shall enter into peace; they shall rest in their beds,
each one walking in his uprightness.*

ISAIAH 57:2

I can't count the number of times recently that women who were once real go-getters—intelligent, creative, and energetic—have said to me that they are just tired of life. They are bored with the humdrum of their daily routines and relationships. They see no way out.

I have two words for that kind of thinking. As the kids in my neighborhood would say, "Chill out." You sound like you're overburdened, brain-dead, and on life support in your mind.

Draw yourself a hot bubble bath tonight and splash around for a while. Thoroughly enjoy the moment. Then, with childlike anticipation, ask your heavenly Father, "Now what?" The answer might be, "Get yourself to bed, woman! You're whipped!" Or it might be something totally outside your routine, like "Go ye into the kitchen at midnight and create for thyself a sundae with every kind of dollop and sprinkle ye can find."

Thelma Wells, *The Great Adventure*

FRESHLY-BAKED CAKE

All things work together for good to those who love God.

ROM. 8:28

I like to compare suffering to making a cake. No one sits down, gets out a box of baking powder, eats a big spoonful, and says, "Hmmm, that's good!" And you don't do that with a spoonful of shortening or raw eggs or flour, either. The tribulation and suffering in our lives can be compared with swallowing a spoonful of baking powder or shortening. By themselves these things are distasteful and they turn your stomach. But God takes all of these ingredients, stirs them up, and puts them in His special oven, thinking *Surely the cake must be done by now.* But not yet, no, not yet. What really matters is that the cake is baking and the marvelous aroma is filling the house.

I find that people who trust God with their suffering have an invisible something, like the aroma of freshly-baked cake, that draws people to them. As Paul put it, "All things [all ingredients of pain and suffering] work together for good to those who love God" (Rom. 8:28 KJV).

Barbara Johnson, *Pack Up Your Gloomees*

I Choose Joy

In Him also we have obtained an inheritance,
being predestined according to the purpose of Him who
works all things according to the counsel of His will.

EPHESIANS 1:11

God, in His sovereign love and power, "works all things after the counsel of His will." My security, my rest, my peace, and my joy live always in the secure knowledge of that comforting truth. But God invites my participation in the executing of His divine will for my life. To me, a part of that participation has to do with how I perceive the events of my life. I determine whether or not I'm going to view my experiences through a negative or positive lens. If indeed my perceptions are negative, then it stands to reason my life will feel out of whack, and . . . I can spend years pouting in my cave. Thank God I don't have to pout, fuss, or complain; I have the option to smile, chuckle, or laugh. When I do, in that arena where God invites my participation, I am in control.

Marilyn Meberg, *Choosing the Amusing*

A Miracle in Disguise

*She brought forth her firstborn son, and wrapped Him
in swaddling cloths, and laid Him in a manger.*

LUKE 2:7

No one was waiting for a Savior in diapers.
No one was looking at a teenage girl to
spill their deliverer out onto straw and hay.

They missed the miracle.

It is outrageous for the Christ whose rightful
place is at the right hand of the Father to step out
of timelessness into say…Tuesday evening, to
exchange the worship of angels for the garb of a
carpenter who wore perhaps…size eleven sandals.

No wonder they missed the miracle. It was so
close to them they almost tripped over it.

Sheila Walsh, *Outrageous Love*

GOD'S LOVE SETS US FREE

*God is love, and he who abides in love
abides in God, and God in him.*

1 JOHN 4:16

We all know the story of the Samaritan woman. Sometimes we don't realize how typical she is of each of us. Surely she longed for a different life, with no hidden places, no secrets, no lying awake at night wondering where it all had gone wrong.

Jesus unlocked her secret with just one statement: "Go and get your husband and come back and we can talk." There it was, out in the sunlight, revealed by Jesus' truthful, but compassionate, words. As she looked at Jesus, the woman realized that she didn't have to run anymore. He knew it all, and yet He loved her. Surely, this Man was a prophet. He had found her hidden places, her addiction to empty relationships. All her life she had looked for someone to fill the void.

The healing light of God's love sets us free.

Sheila Walsh, *Life Is Tough but God Is Faithful*

PRAYING WITH PURPOSE

*For this reason we also, since the day we heard it,
do not cease to pray for you, and to ask
that you may be filled with the knowledge of His will
in all wisdom and spiritual understanding.*

COLOSSIANS 1:9

Praying with purpose is powerful. Asking for godly behavior and character in the people you love is one of the sweetest gifts you can give them.

Praying with purpose is persistent. If you are going to pray for someone and expect God to move, your persistence says to Him, "I really want this, and I am counting on You to do it."

Praying with purpose will become your passion when you begin to see how the heart of God is moved, when you take prayer as seriously as He does.

Jan Silvious, *Women of Faith Devotional Bible*

The Road of Life

The LORD is my strength and my song,
and He has become my salvation.

EXODUS 15:2

Life is full of experiences that challenge, confound, and concern us—and create circumstances that cause the road in front of us to take turns we don't anticipate or welcome. We get news we didn't want and can't send back by overnight mail. Family situations are strained. We feel as though even our best friends don't understand what we're going through. Life feels so tough sometimes that we wish we were dead. I know. I've been there.

But I've also been there for the resurrection moments. Just when I feel I can't take one more second in the black hole of my own hope-starved soul, God shows up in ways I don't anticipate. I get "zapped" by a jolt of encouragement on the side of the road. I discover treasure instead of torment. The bottom drops out and I land in the palm of God's hand.

Thelma Wells, *The Great Adventure*

LEARNING TO DEPEND ON GOD

*In the time of trouble He shall hide me
in His pavilion; in the secret place of His tabernacle.*

PSALM 27:5

Taking a fork in the road spells "adventure" to some and "danger" to others of us who appreciate predictability, even if it is a measurable rut. Learning to be adventuresome again included lessons for me on taking the risk of trusting others, the Lord, and myself.

I gained strength for the challenge as I studied the lives of God's people, people who shook in their sandals and yet still obeyed God's direction. When they came to a fork in the road, they depended on Him to direct their steps, whether they found themselves in a desert, a furnace, a prison, or a shipwreck. And there were those who were too afraid initially to take God at His word: the Gideons and the Peters. Yet God gathered their weakness into His strength and sent them forth with courage. That gives me hope that even in my most inadequate moments the Lord still reigns over my life.

Patsy Clairmont, *The Great Adventure*

"WE THANK YOU!"

Give unto the LORD the glory due to His name;
worship the LORD in the beauty of holiness.

PSALM 29:1

Expressing our gratitude to God is a rich
adventure in itself. After all, think about what
we've been delivered from. We've been rescued
from the cold night of sin that alienates us from
God. We were like strays struggling to keep warm,
to find a place of shelter from the icy blast of life.
We were homeless and helpless, wounded and
broken, marked by the scars of life. God in His
overwhelming love sent Jesus to woo us back to
Himself. He has paid for our healing; He fed us
and loved us back to life. Now, a sweet part of our
adventure here on earth is to live a life of gratitude.
To look for creative ways of telling our awesome
God, "We love you! We thank you!
We will live for you!"

Sheila Walsh,
The Great Adventure

A Plan for the Future

He will teach us His ways,
and we shall walk in His paths.

MICAH 4:2

I want a reason to get up in the morning. When I ask God for a sense of personal destiny, and then listen carefully, I get a sense of direction. Not always, and not always immediately, but I rely on God's promises to consistently guide me toward fulfilling the purpose for which He created me.

I love the fact that God has a plan for the future, for every tomorrow of my life on earth and beyond. Even though I can't figure it all out, He's got it wired. This reassures me that I'm loved and safe. God knows our course and He knows us. He loves us. He provides. He plans ahead.

Luci Swindoll, *I Married Adventure*

Grateful acknowledgment is made to the following publishers for permission to reprint this copyrighted material.

Lana Bateman ©, *The Heart of Prayer* (Nashville: J Countryman, 2004).

Dee Brestin and Kathy Troccoli ©, *The Colors of His Love* (Nashville: W. Publishing Group, 2002)

Jill Briscoe ©, *Here am I, Lord, . . . Send Somebody Else* (Nashville: W Publishing Group, 2004)

Patsy Clairmont ©, *The Shoe Box* (Nashville: W. Publishing Group, 2003)

Patsy Clairmont ©, *The Hat Box* (Nashville: W. Publishing Group, 2003)

Patsy Clairmont et al. ©, *The Great Adventure* (Nashville: W. Publishing Group, 2002)

Barbara Johnson ©, *Stick a Geranium in Your Hat and Be Happy* (Nashville: W. Publishing Group, 1990).

Barbara Johnson ©, *Pack Up Your Gloomies in a Great Big Box* (Nashville: W. Publishing Group, 1993).

Barbara Johnson ©, *Mamma, Get the Hammer!* (Nashville: W. Publishing Group, 1994).

Barbara Johnson ©, *Living Somewhere Between Estrogen and Death* (Nashville: W. Publishing Group, 1997).

Barbara Johnson ©, *He's Gonna Toot, and I'm Gonna Scoot* (Nashville: W. Publishing Group, 1999).

Barbara Johnson ©, *Leaking Laffs Between Pampers and Depends* (Nashville: W. Publishing Group, 2000).

Nicole Johnson ©, *Fresh-Brewed Life* (Nashville: W. Publishing Group, 1999)

Nicole Johnson ©, *Keeping a Princess Heart* (Nashville: W. Publishing Group, 2003)

Marilyn Meberg ©, *Choosing the Amusing* (Nashville: W. Publishing Group, 1999)

Marilyn Meberg ©, *The Zippered Heart* (Nashville: W. Publishing Group, 2001)

Marilyn Meberg ©, *The Decision of a Lifetime* (Nashville: W. Publishing Group, 2003)

Marilyn Meberg ©, *Overcoming Mistakes* (Nashville: Thomas Nelson, Inc., 2004)

Marilyn Meberg ©, *Assurance for a Lifetime* (Nashville: W. Publishing Group, 2004)

Marilyn Meberg ©, *Overcoming Difficulties* (Nashville: Thomas Nelson, Inc., 2004)

Jan Silvious ©, *Big Girls Don't Whine* (Nashville: W. Publishing Group, 2003)

Luci Swindoll ©, *You Bring the Confetti* (Nashville: W. Publishing Group, 1986)

Luci Swindoll ©, *I Married Adventure* (Nashville: W. Publishing Group, 2002)

Kathy Troccoli ©, *Hope for a Woman's Heart* (Nashville: J Countryman, 2002).

Sheila Walsh ©, *Life Is Tough but God Is Faithful* (Nashville: Thomas Nelson, Inc., 1999)

Sheila Walsh ©, *The Heartache No One Sees* (Nashville: Thomas Nelson, Inc., 2004)

Sheila Walsh ©, *Outrageous Love* (Nashville: J Countryman, 2004)

Thelma Wells ©, *Girl, Have I Got Good News for You* (Nashville: W Publishing Group, 2000)

Women of Faith ©, *Women of Faith Devotional Bible* (Nashville: Thomas Nelson Bibles, 2003)

Women of Faith ©, *Laughter Is the Spice of Life* (Nashville: W. Publishing Group, 2004).

Women of Faith ©, *Women of Faith Study Guide Series,* Christa Kinde, ed. Adventurous Prayer (Nashville: Thomas Nelson, Inc., 2003).

Women of Faith ©, *Women of Faith Study Guide Series,* Christa Kinde, ed. Discovering God's will for Your Life (Nashville: Thomas Nelson, Inc., 2003).

Women of Faith ©, Women of Faith Study Guide Series, Christa Kinde, ed., *Living Above Worry and Stress* (Nashville: Thomas Nelson, Inc., 2003).

Women of Faith ©, Women of Faith Study Guide Series, Christa Kinde, ed. *Living in Jesus* (Nashville: Thomas Nelson, Inc., 2003).

Women of Faith ©, Women of Faith Study Guide Series, Christa Kinde, ed. *A Life of Worship* (Nashville: Thomas Nelson, Inc., 2004).

Women of Faith ©, Women of Faith Study Guide Series, Christa Kinde, ed. *Cultivating Contentment* (Nashville: Thomas Nelson, Inc., 2004).

Women of Faith ©, Women of Faith Study Guide Series, Christa Kinde, ed. *Encouraging One Another* (Nashville: Thomas Nelson, Inc., 2004).

Women of Faith ©, Women of Faith Study Guide Series, Christa Kinde, ed. *Managing Your Moods* (Nashville: Thomas Nelson, Inc., 2004).

MISSION STATEMENT

OUR VISION

Women of Faith's vision is to see women
set free to a lifestyle of God's grace

OUR MISSION

Women of Faith's mission is to host events and create
resources that nurture women spiritually,
emotionally, and in their relationships with others

OUR CORE VALUES

The transforming power of grace

Striving for excellence

Honoring God and His people

The power of story and the healing of humor

Modeling community

Living in faith

OUR MESSAGE

Women of Faith communicates God's
unconditional love regardless of religious affiliation

MINISTRY PARTNERS

CAMPUS CRUSADE FOR CHRIST

Campus Crusade for Christ International is an interdenominational
ministry committed to helping take the gospel of Jesus Christ to all nations.
Campus Crusade has partnered with Women of Faith to provide resources
for women to grow in their faith. *ccci.org*

INTEGRITY MUSIC

In partnership with Women of Faith, Integrity Music produces the music sung
at the conferences (CDs and songbooks). Their mission is to help people
worldwide experience the presence of God. *integritymusic.com*

THOMAS NELSON PUBLISHERS

Women of Faith, a division of Thomas Nelson Publishing, produces books, Bibles
and ministry resources in partnership with J Countryman, Nelson Bibles, Nelson
Books, Nelson Reference & Electronic Publishing, Tommy Nelson, and W Publishing
Group. The Women of Faith product line is specifically designed to help encourage
women and their families spiritually, emotionally and relationally. *thomasnelson.com*

WOMEN OF FAITH ASSOCIATION

Enjoy fellowship with other Women of Faith members around the world, find
encouragement for everyday challenges and be encouraged when you need
God's guidance most. *womenoffaith.com/association*

WORLD VISION

Help a child, a family, even a whole village in the developing world
for just a few cents a day. Visit the World Vision resource table on the
concourse or get information at *worldvision.org*.

EXTRAORDINARY*faith*
CONFERENCE 2005

2005 EVENT CITIES & SPECIAL GUESTS

NATIONAL CONFERENCE
LAS VEGAS, NV
FEBRUARY 17-19
Thomas & Mack Center

NATIONAL CONFERENCE
FT. LAUDERDALE, FL
FEBRUARY 24-26
Office Depot Center

SHREVEPORT, LA
APRIL 1-2
CenturyTel Center
Sandi Patty, Chonda Pierce, Jennifer Rothschild

HOUSTON, TX
APRIL 8-9
Toyota Center
Kristin Chenoweth, Natalie Grant, Jennifer Rothschild

COLUMBUS, OH
APRIL 15-16
Nationwide Arena
Avalon, Kristin Chenoweth, Nichole Nordeman

BILLINGS, MT
MAY 13-14
MetraPark
Sandi Patty, Chonda Pierce, Jennifer Rothschild

PITTSBURGH, PA
MAY 20-21
Mellon Arena
Natalie Grant, Nichole Nordeman, Chonda Pierce

KANSAS CITY, MO
JUNE 3-4
Kemper Arena
Natalie Grant, Chonda Pierce, Jennifer Rothschild

ST. LOUIS, MO
JUNE 17-18
Savvis Center
Avalon, Nichole Nordeman, Chonda Pierce

CANADA & NEW ENGLAND CRUISE
JUNE 25 – JULY 2
Tammy Trent

ATLANTA, GA
JULY 8-9
Philips Arena
Natalie Grant, Sherri Shepherd, Tammy Trent

FT. WAYNE, IN
JULY 15-16
Allen County War Memorial Coliseum
Sandi Patty, Chonda Pierce, Jennifer Rothschild

DETROIT, MI
JULY 22-23
Palace of Auburn Hills
Sherri Shepherd, Tammy Trent, CeCe Winans

WASHINGTON, DC
JULY 29-30
MCI Center
Natalie Grant, Nichole Nordeman, Sherri Shepherd

SACRAMENTO, CA
AUGUST 5-6
ARCO Arena
Avalon, Kristin Chenoweth, Tammy Trent

PORTLAND, OR
AUGUST 12-13
Rose Garden Arena
Kristin Chenoweth, Natalie Grant, Tammy Trent

DENVER, CO
AUGUST 19-20
Pepsi Center
Avalon, Kristin Chenoweth, Nichole Nordeman

DALLAS, TX
AUGUST 26-27
American Airlines Center
Avalon, Kristin Chenoweth, Nichole Nordeman

ANAHEIM, CA
SEPTEMBER 9-10
Arrowhead Pond
Avalon, Chonda Pierce, Tammy Trent

PHILADELPHIA, PA
SEPTEMBER 16-17
Wachovia Center
Kathie Lee Gifford, Natalie Grant, Nichole Nordeman

ALBANY, NY
SEPTEMBER 23-24
Pepsi Arena
Sandi Patty, Chonda Pierce

HARTFORD, CT
SEPT. 30 – OCT. 1
Hartford Civic Center
Sandi Patty, Chonda Pierce, Tammy Trent

SEATTLE, WA
OCTOBER 7-8
Key Arena
Sandi Patty, Chonda Pierce, Jennifer Rothschild

DES MOINES, IA
OCTOBER 14-15
Wells Fargo Arena
Sandi Patty, Chonda Pierce, Jennifer Rothschild

ST. PAUL, MN
OCTOBER 21-22
Xcel Energy Center
Sandi Patty, Chonda Pierce, Jennifer Rothschild

CHARLOTTE, NC
OCTOBER 28-29
Charlotte Coliseum
Sandi Patty, Beth Moore, Sherri Shepherd

OKLAHOMA CITY, OK
NOVEMBER 4-5
Ford Center
Kristin Chenoweth, Sandi Patty, Chonda Pierce

ORLANDO, FL
NOVEMBER 11-12
TD Waterhouse Centre
Avalon, Chonda Pierce, Tammy Trent

1-888-49-FAITH womenoffaith.com

Guests subject to change. Not all guests appear in every city. Visit womenoffaith.com for details on special guests, registration deadlines and pricing.

MARILYN MEBERG

God at Your Wits End

"I know God loves me, but does He like me?" "Are my prayers not answered because I don't have enough faith?" These questions and more plague our minds and weaken our faith. *God at Your Wits' End* probes our minds to uncover faulty thinking that leads to an uncertain faith. But author Marilyn Meberg doesn't leave us there — she brings us hope as she helps us reshape our thinking and re-establish the foundations of our belief in a loving God. Theme book of the 2005 Women of Faith Pre-conference of the same name.

SHEILA WALSH

Extraordinary Faith

We all face situations that we cannot control. All we can do is trust — and have faith — that God will see us through. Best-selling author and Women of Faith speaker Sheila Walsh shares insights on the simple life-giving gift God offers His children — the gift of faith. By sharing biblical and modern examples of women of faith, Sheila opens our eyes to the extravagant gift God has for each of us. Theme book of the 2005 Women of Faith conference.